MW00978697

Much
Love
Carrie

More Than Existing

CORRIE THORNE

BALBOA.PRESS

A DIVISION OF HAY HOUSE

Copyright © 2020 Corrie Thorne.

Edited by Lisa Richard

All rights reserved. No part of this book may be used or reproduced by any means, graphic, electronic, or mechanical, including photocopying, recording, taping or by any information storage retrieval system without the written permission of the author except in the case of brief quotations embodied in critical articles and reviews.

Balboa Press books may be ordered through booksellers or by contacting:

Balboa Press
A Division of Hay House
1663 Liberty Drive
Bloomington, IN 47403
www.balboapress.com
1 (877) 407-4847

Because of the dynamic nature of the Internet, any web addresses or links contained in this book may have changed since publication and may no longer be valid. The views expressed in this work are solely those of the author and do not necessarily reflect the views of the publisher, and the publisher hereby disclaims any responsibility for them.

The author of this book does not dispense medical advice or prescribe the use of any technique as a form of treatment for physical, emotional, or medical problems without the advice of a physician, either directly or indirectly. The intent of the author is only to offer information of a general nature to help you in your quest for emotional and spiritual well-being. In the event you use any of the information in this book for yourself, which is your constitutional right, the author and the publisher assume no responsibility for your actions.

Any people depicted in stock imagery provided by Getty Images are models, and such images are being used for illustrative purposes only. Certain stock imagery © Getty Images.

Print information available on the last page.

ISBN: 978-1-9822-5085-0 (sc)
ISBN: 978-1-9822-5086-7 (hc)
ISBN: 978-1-9822-5087-4 (e)

Library of Congress Control Number: 2020912889

Balboa Press rev. date: 07/24/2020

CONTENTS

ACKNOWLEDGEMENT

I begin with a thank you to the creator, source, the light of the god consciousness within, whom without my life as I know it to be, would not exist. Thank you to Jesus, Mother Mary, the angels and the guides who have held me to my faith and reminded me to always return to the faith in myself. For even after I have been in the shadows of my darker days, I would be taken to a vision of the light.

I give love, appreciation and blessings to my parents who have loved me by choice. For always being open and real to their beautiful imperfections and with gratitude for always teaching me to do what was morally right, installing an understanding of the importance of integrity and dignity. To my daughter and now to be arriving first granddaughter, my greatest teacher, accomplishment and the reason why healing the past and breaking the cycles was an important part of the journey I would need to endure. To my patient and accepting life partner, and the love that has been ever evolving and growing within me as I have learned through his eyes the true meaning of acceptance, I say thank you. My brother, thank you for the stories and for being the best brother, words that only the grownup me can say as the truest of truth. I am grateful for a stepmother who has always loved my dad and his kind heart. A sister-in law who became one of my best friends and provided support throughout the years, blessing our world with the favourite men in my life, my nephews. I have been truly blessed with the perfect (for me) family who is real, true, combined and infused with love as we all come together so perfectly. To my ancestors and extended family, I am blessed and say thank you for providing me the guidance to bring my life out of the shadows and into a light of love, reminding me that we are human but that the bad behaviour is never acceptable, and that forgiveness always sets us free from our own misery and suffering.

To all of the relationships who have been in my stories I say thank you. From a place of self awareness, I know that in every relationship exists my own responsibility to take in the roles I played and trust that my heart has a right to the memories as they were experienced in my view. To my daughter's stepfather, for choosing to love her as his own and for the continual support, thank you. To Louise Hay and Doctor Wayne Dyer from their time on earth and the guidance from beyond I have learned love, trust, faith and in so many ways they have given me reminders to never give up! To the powerful goddesses, Jennifer, Demi, Shakira, Tina, Cher, and Miss Piggy, thank you for the inspiration, along with Crystal Andres Morrissette for coaching and guiding me to step up my game and my life. Allison Lund and Lisa Star Francis, thank you for being friends and colleagues, and for giving me the reminders and kicks in the ass to push beyond what I believed I was capable of when in my lowest days. Thank you for always leading the way for strong powerful women to stand up and be true to themselves. To Mother Teresa, Martin Luther King, and all who have walked the line of judgement remaining firm in the conviction to the truth, and the rights and freedoms that we are all equal and loving humans with a mission to live our dreams, while remembering to also care for and support our human race. A reminder that the change starts with us, through a commitment to try and do the right thing. To all who have lent me their eyes to see, I say thank you. To my friends who have stood by my side and the soul sisters in my life I am humbled by the love and support. To my sisters by choice thank you for being a part of my stories. To those who have challenged and judged me, I say thank you for reflecting back at me the things within myself that I didn't want to see when I looked in my own mirror at night. My heart of acknowledgement goes to the children of my friends who have had to leave this world too soon, as I remember the blessings of the breath I get to take and the opportunities and time I have with those I love is a blessing. To my dedicated angel on earth and friend Lisa I am not sure there are enough words! Thank you.

INTRODUCTION

More Than Existing has been written as if I have already made it. Made it to achieving a level of spiritual growth that has given me a rite of passage to a new life, or better yet to the life I designed before I arrived. I will speak of myself as if the past I have lived bears no weight into the future I am living, and that my days are not filled with self-doubt and fear, but inspiration and unconditional love for the woman I have become.

It started with a desire in my heart for a return to something I had yet to feel or experience within this lifetime until now. "I am done," were the words that would fall over my lips and onto the paper as if a staff had hit the ground, the earth shook, and I was waiting for the waters to part. The truth was the water fell as tears from my eyes and hit the page like heavy rain weighted with heavy energy. They hit and splattered over the words and as I watched the ink spread, I knew in my heart that this time my words were heard and with an uneasy feeling I turned the page and set out on a journey to discover a life of *More Than Existing*.

I was driven by a force that would question my faith and turn the world as I knew it upside down. I can tell you I have no regrets for the choice to write these words and today I am honored to share my journey with you.

I invite you to close your eyes, and take in a deep breath, before we start this journey together. Then for just a moment, imagine watching your life as if you are seeing an old movie displayed reel by reel, but with no break and no place to stop and sit. Just a role of life that flickers by so that you can connect to the moments and memories.

I will infuse the channeled messages with my own stories throughout this book and all that I shall write will be a web of messages from the spiritual essence of the Channel who speaks through me and the human I am fully embracing today. I am a mystic, a prophetess, a channel to the Divine and most of all I am human, please do not mistake me for a doctor, psychologist or as anyone's guru. I am a professional life coach and a spiritual teacher, teaching through sharing my stories and how moving past the filters and lenses on our eyes came through for me. I ask of you to not sit in judgement, regret, denial, and fear. Let it all slip by with a little smile on your face that you have made it to this point and that you are so very okay and safe in this moment that we are sitting in.

Before we start, please remember as with all stories this is the truth of only my own recollection as seen through the eyes and felt through the heart during that stage in my journey of trying to more than exist. We all have our versions and our stories. Your life and the healing journey of this life may change as you grow and excel to a new level on a journey that you never lost, we just forget to walk in our grace.

This life is yours to live and your story is somewhat yours to tell. In writing this book and going through the process of creation, it has reminded me of how we all have a story and a version that makes our world comfortable to live in the uncomfortable, until the day we choose to set ourselves free.

Today I live as simply just me! A woman who had a desire to set herself free! And now, let's begin the journey from shadow self to true self.

CHAPTER 1

I have been given the key

I am done! I am discovering happiness
and joy no matter the cost.

I AM THE ESSENCE OF my existence and the cause of my continued issues. I am responsible and accountable for my life as I know it to be today, and anything happening within me I am now allowing. I am making a choice to ignore and neglect the truths I do not want to face. What happens if I am to face a truth that I then have to live with? I guess we will have to see!

Will I be brave enough to stand tall in the light and be seen as my raw, real, and vulnerable true self? As I show myself mercy and step out of the protective armor I had worn for so many years, will I truly be able to walk out and be free? Free from my own bondage of the illusions of my truth, the stories, and lies that held me captive for so long. As I think of myself, and those I show mercy and compassion to, along with their mistreatments of me or those around me, I feel every one of these individuals are the reflection of myself I had been making excuses for. If I made excuses for them, I was making excuses for me. Wow! What a lie I had been living in, to have never realized that the lenses I was looking through this whole time were a reflection of me and my life.

Through the eyes of even those who abused my soul emotionally, and whether it had been carried out intentionally or unintentionally, I was ultimately responsible for letting them in and allowing the behavior to continue with a belief that at some point if they changed, I would be at peace. The truth was that if they did change, it would be because they made the choice to change, and I was then just reaping in the rewards of their win. I would still be searching for another piece to not be okay. Who would I be, without waiting for the tower moment of death and destruction, of when the essence of me would then not be enough? I had played and toyed around with the game of Russian roulette for long enough within this life. I have been a storywriter and teller, queen of lies, and faces of masks for so long that my fear of the truth has become crippling to me.

The cost of living has cost me everything I could not afford to lose, but God has given me many golden gifts and for that I say, "Thank you." Sometimes you just cannot see the gifts. From this point on, I sit in the experience of ultimate joy and happiness, and as I always say, "You can't make this shit up!" I was about to start this book through the pain, but a call had come in and distracted my very thought, a call that my future grandchild will be a little girl. I sit with my salty tears and a heart I cannot contain. From beginning to end, in this book my one true joy has always been my daughter, who is now carrying the next generation of strong powerful women. This book is written with my future granddaughter in mind. She is worthy of the cycles being broken, but with faith in the process that the cycle of strong women in our lives today be the ones to break that cycle, starting with me.

I now sit at a scarred desk caused from holding vigil for a beautiful young woman who is courageously battling her way through her journey of pain, making us question God and the why of it all. The power of the flame shattering through the glass vase, and leaving its mark upon on the desk. I am reminded of my rise from the ashes, opening me up to the awareness of the honor I feel as I sit in grace, the clairvoyant in me can clearly see the unfolding of the future events of this movement we are now in the wake of experiencing. I graciously and humbly ask of you to be open and compassionate to my truth as it has been received by all versions of me and the messages from channel I have been asked to communicate through my beliefs and faith. I am sorry if they offend, but the I AM of truth to my existence is not without my connection to the Holy Council of Jesus, Mother Mary and all whom I will speak of, I do not exist, like a mixed blend of spice favorable to some but not to all. I now take you on my journey of *More Than Existing*.

I had become what I thought was forever broken by a moment of making a hard decision and sacrificing a precious gift of my soul. As my body hit a level of trauma and pain that I am unsure words exist to describe but can still be felt by an empath. With a now, in shock and dead sense of self, I had aborted my child and sold my soul for the cost of contentment in the life of another. I stood and walked out through the doors of judgement and signs of hate. It was an ending and a beginning into a realization that all of my life had been under an illusion of just existing. The strangers of a so-called faith to love all, stoned me with their words and I quickly forgave, for I knew I could not carry the burden in my heart, but I had forgiven all but one, myself! My journey to the depths of my shadows began here, but it is not the creation of the shadows, that sadly goes deeper.

This is not as it shall begin, this was the moment of awakening, which is nothing like the movies of sparkles and butterflies. This is my truth and it is not to shock but to awaken us to the pain, shame, and secrets we hide and have for a lifetime. It was the appearance of the hands of Mother Mary and the direction she had taken me to the cross, placing the crown of thorns on the head of Jesus. The look in his eyes showing me his pain gave me the courage to walk through the paths that I would take. My moments of reflection had just begun. It has taken faith to show me the light in the dark, to find the courage it takes to say "No," when something does not align to your soul and that your "Yes," should always be of your own accord. Faith to walk as a leader, who is a follower, but willing to walk into the unknown to shine a light for those to come.

Life had become more like, a nutcracker tool to a nut! Apply enough pressure and tension and it will eventually break. The shattered pieces hitting the floor exposing the nut to be created in many forms, crunched up and swallowed into the darkness. Yes, this is how my brain works, you will discover I am the child of a mother with attention deficit hyperactivity disorder (ADHD), and we have learned this is a beautiful part of the gift, so let's stick together. My situations are far from humorous, but my survival has been based on it and yes that may have been conditioned to me. Before you judge, listen to what you hear as if it were your own words, that they may echo back the words of your story, as I place my vulnerable self out in this book for you to read. This is the story of a child, a daughter, a mother, a now soon to be grandmother, a woman, and a CEO! It is the story of a human who forgot her human.

Just as in the church, as I had watched my grandmother place her little sealed envelope, here I was sitting within my own feminine temple with an offering placed by my coffee cup. I sat and asked the question for one last time, "God is this mine to take?" I had been gifted not only this new lease on life but the money to finally start publishing the creation of my existence and the vulnerable reality of the human experience. Yet sure of the words, I still had a moment of questioning my worthiness. It was hard enough when the first gift of money came from another with a love for me and the messages of my heart. His voice was strong and sturdy, as it is when he has a message to convey, "My only option was golden, and I had to go for gold." I was still unsure of the faith in myself, but I started to walk the next stage of the journey. I am uncertain if he knew the message he had conveyed at the time, but his offering I was sure had been made of faith and love. As to what I thought was to be, the ending of the book unfolded, and I became aware of the ultimate sacrifice that was beyond the archetype of any form of Jesus. It was the sacrifice of the God consciousness, the energy that made a choice to drop into us all to experience all that was possible of creation, to form into existence.

There was magic, freewill, and all that was to be experienced was ours as a race to create. That light giving safety to surrender and placing trust in us to learn, to grow, and to thrive. I had to stop choking myself off from the Source to breathe this new life, and to open back up to connect to the source of existence, to then know what an honor has been bestowed upon us. Was I really going to throw that gift away? I could not end this journey without coming into the essence of God and all that has transpired within my life. I have been the witness to so many of life's experiences but have remained humble enough to know that this life has much more for me to yet experience. I am alive and awake, with eyes wide open I can now see but yet I am still blind. As the world before me has not yet evolved, to all that the Prophet inside of me can now see in faith. I am a SEER and I well understand a world of destruction and dismantling will always have to be, just as death and rebirth will always bring forth new life. The fear I once lived, still appears as a reminder of the human that capsules my spirit, but now my soul is free. I can forgive, for those who attack are baring a cross and as I sit at their feet how can I not have compassion for their pain. I have set myself free from many of the crosses but it was not until I was ready to sit at my own feet that I was able to see the ultimate sacrifice the Source of it all made for my experience upon this earth.

I have met all that I am today by meeting and accepting all that I see through the eyes of those who have walked and will walk upon this earth. The judgement, the angers, the desires to be right, the secrets and fears of dismantling to awaken the truths. The desire to convince ourselves that pain and suffering is our place of comfort, or that the punishment we lash out upon ourselves is acceptable, while we cringe in anger for seeing others wrongly punished. The desire to find joy and happiness has cost me everything, but what I have gained in return, is beyond words as I discovered that the dictionary lies about the meaning of words. Here I insert a big chuckle, because the dictionary did not tell me "Joy" would take me to the depth of darkness, into the soul of my good, bad, and the ugly, only to reappear into the light with a realization that most of my life has been an illusion and creation of my own choice. A choice to continue to believe the truth of those who are still not awakened to a life without fear, instead of always placing faith in the Divine. Yes, I am very aware that we have grief and suffered at the hands of others and that some losses are almost impossible to bare, but I am still breathing, and my light is still very alive. As is the light of those around us, for now I truly understand the phrase, "The spirit in me, sees the spirit in you." That the return to love is truly a humble moment experienced through the eyes of humility to see my greatness and graciously accepting the offering and sacrifices that had been made for me. To not just walk this earth, but to journey through this life. I am humbled by all that has transpired over the eleven years it has taken to write this book and am in awe of the love and compassion I have experienced from those who have lent me their eyes so that I could see. To those who are offering and sacrificed their time to read this book, to those who signed the contracts, to others who at some point will walk this journey and be a part of any or all my experience. From the place I sit,

I humbly know I hold my key to unlock the door to a life of *More Than Existing*. The golden key is in all the layers unfolding as we continue through the mind of the mystic, prophet, and most of all the human that I am today.

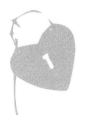

CHAPTER 2

The reunion of my soul

I NEEDED A HUMBLING BUT was not prepared for the crash landing of the grounding. I felt as if my human self was in a place of ego which I call fear. I was in a place of self-awareness, a coma of knowing but not listening. Spiraling out of the vortex of alignment and into the deep darkness of fear and self-sabotage. I had become so humanly connected to an outcome I so badly wanted, that I had lost sight of all that I needed to be, the essence of the whole version of me.

My desire for external love and attention became the everything of my day and based on everything I had experienced from the past. I had come so far but was yet still so lost. My all-knowing wisdom was so aware and I had such a desire to be that of the Holy's but was still sabotaging and punishing the human self with a desire for all that I knew to not be real, but an illusion of the stockpile of lies I had been conditioned to live, and believed still had a place at the front of the line. I had done the damn work, studied the books, became the master, the teacher, fuck I had done it all and here I was once again on the edge of ascension and determined to look back down. What if there was one more last word, last regret, last punishment I should experience? What would those I was leaving behind do without me, the Mothership I had become? This is not by anyone's definition but of my own accord as I was fearful of all that I had asked for, the ultimate experience of love, a marriage of two souls.

I am on the home stretch to acquire that last key, as if I am in the amazing race waiting to hear I made it. But here I am on my knees in a truth I was choosing to not escape, why? Where or how did this desire to be accepted find its way in? How did I lose the faith in something I knew so well? I had become human. I had actually for a moment, let go of the wheel I had been clutching so hard, afraid of falling, and afraid of what was coming, that I let go at the first bump instead of letting myself ride to the moments ahead. You see, I put an obstacle in the way allowing my self-sabotage moment to appear.

This was my opportunity to return to the moment of trust and faith in humanity that went through the door as I had watched my dad so many years before sell himself short and put his trust and faith in those who intentionally preyed on his weakness as a business man. His naivety and kindness to the cruel intentions of others was his weakness. I was still falling victim to so many stories of humility, defined by the definition in the human dictionary, and not having the courage to look with humility at my own weaknesses. As a part of the sense of all of the versions of me that had been trailing through my existence, my desire to be free, had held me captive to a truth that trusting the person I was yet to know was virtually impossible. My shadow was telling me a lie and I had become someone who had more faith in a lie because I was holding onto hope. I could use this as my story of, why try? Choose the safe route, go back to the job that was safe and I knew so well. I could sit in the comfortable and say, "Oh well I missed this opportunity so I will wait until the next one." Really? Is that really the shit that Corrie lives or teaches? No, but I was in a space and a place that I needed to feel to relive the sense of vulnerability that had been sheltered away behind my role as a spiritual healer/teacher, who forgot to continue to place herself up into a standard of importance.

I had a realization of my reality that came after the realization of the truth in my reality. Confusing? Imagine being in this head always living in multiple states of reality and still seeking refuge from the trauma and disappointment of human behaviors, and I am not just talking about others! I am speaking of my own behaviors and fear of why I should push aside those who want to walk beside me. My partnerships of loyalty and trust had rarely matched the love in my heart I gave out, and making me appear less than had been a promising story of growth and glory for others. That is a truth but not a reality, as I am sitting and feeling blessed that I have become aware that I could not save a burning house that was meant to burn. I could sense another humbling appearing and the discovery that I should not speak to anyone when in a state of explosive of the old self.

As I unravel, I reel in and from a place of humiliation I learn humility. The first partnership I failed was the one with me as I was well taught that I did not matter. That awareness could only arrive in the phoenix moment of humbling, which came from the story of the burnt desk in chapter one. I guess here I should explain a little more of the experience I spoke of and as mystical and beautiful as the phoenix may be, the experience was anything but. When we begin an awakening, the dying process begins and this was not my first go around with the thought of real death, or the process of the dying away of the old self. That moment was after a few weeks of a new level of pain where I truly felt I could not go on any longer. Then a few messages came in as I was driving home from visiting my own doctor from some of the beautiful people who follow my work and who were in need of my prayers through their fight with pain on all levels. In that moment I took the focus off of how I was going to get out of this world and placed my focus on the beautiful people courageously reaching out to ask for prayers of strength, hope, and love from a person they have come to trust but did not personally know.

That evening I sat in prayer with the candle on my desk, holy water to one side and statue of Mother Mary on the other until a voice said, "Go rest and let the flame burn." I fell into a deep sleep and as you will read of the Mary's holding my hands, I was guided to not look back as I heard my name but could not leave the promise of continuing to look forward, I slept through the warning that the smell of smoke brings. Awakening to a house full of smoke and a burnt desk that should have gone up in flames, I sat with tears in my eyes and remembered what I had been walking towards in my dreams. I had seen an image of Jesus in the flames and I knew I was to have faith in something I believed but was still unwilling to surrender to it all. As I sat in a flood of tears, I looked at the pieces of broken glass and heard, "Your light is too bright to be contained, leave those people to us, their pain you cannot carry." With a faith now in my heart, I continued to hold space and not their pain. The moment I was still too humble to see until later on, when working through a coaching session where I finally came to the realization that "I matter!"

I was falling and even though I was still strong enough to reach out to help others, I was not strong enough to reach out and ask for my own healing. That day I saved myself and became my saviour. I was now once again reborn, and never will I speak of leaving this earth by my own doing again. My reminders are in the eyes of those fighting so hard to stay and through my eyes I was providing hope but was determined to give away my light to save another. Thinking back and moving forward with my story I am walking forward, still a little behind the Mary's, being reminded over the past few weeks that even the queen will fall but a humble servant will forever walk the path side by side with those who archetype the resemblance to the awakened and aware, and the wakened and unaware. But mostly we are always walking with the human and that in itself is a humbling when we become aware and small and understand how little we truly know.

The moment I became small was the day I allowed myself to fall from the crown of thorns, that has now been dismantled and burned. The need for a crown shall be no more, but a cloak and a staff have taken its place and I with honour am now truly ready to walk the archetype of Moses and lead slightly ahead to break ground and hold space, but not far enough that it leaves room for the enemy to sneak in. I am now walking a life that has humbled me to my knees and this is the place I had to be to finally sense the joy, without letting the faith or the "why" become watered down. The commandments of my life are simple, and alignment is finally becoming an image I can now understand. The pathway to the light and the rush and desire to get "somewhere" is ultimately death. It is the end and as much as we all want to achieve the awards, praise, and validation we often forget to live. We breathe, we rush around, we even forget to say "hello" sometimes. We have an existence, a plan, and we lay a foundation for empires to build on. But those desires are fueled by a false reality, and all too often a false confidence, and as with my story this becomes an all too relatable story for so many who have experienced the rise and fall of many an empire.

CHAPTER 3

What is the cost of your freedom?

JUST WHEN I THOUGHT I was at the end of the *More Than Existing* journey I realized I had only just begun. I wanted to be free! I wanted to be done. I had been so depleted and exhausted and had become very aware of my own decision to find happiness and joy, and yes at all cost! As much as I was experiencing it in the presence of my external life in flickers and moments, it was also in my prayers and meditation. It was so far from my inner existence that I found myself begging to be set free and aware that the cost of my freedom is not as that of so many.

I received a humbling and awareness to what it means to pay the ultimate price as I spent a week during the American Thanksgiving weekend in Reno, Nevada and arrived at the full awareness and understanding of the "why" of the trip. This humbling experience took me to a new place in my heart, and yes we all know the stories of war and the soldiers you've read about, but to actually sit with the soldiers, to be a part of something that only they would know as their eyes meet, and to experience standing in front of a Christmas tree dedicated to those who had paid the ultimate price made writing this next section seem selfish of me. However this next section is still part of my story and commitment that I now hold as my contract in making choices that align to living as if I am blessed, and always honoring the cost that was paid for our freedom and safety. This is no longer about agreeing or disagreeing with war, this is about the human, so be aware of where your ego takes you as you read this part and every part of the writings.

"In accordance with the laws of my highest self and the law of God, I declare an oath to walk in the grace of my golden light, with mercy for myself and others."

This contract I had received from the guides and angels and now hold dear, dedicating to a friend, who because of his rank is among the few who get to call me by my given name.

I randomly had the spirit world of soldiers appear as I stood in front of that Christmas tree and found myself being guided to pass on their messages to strangers all gathering in this casino, as if that place had become their church, a place of congregation, an escape. I am unsure in the moment, but my heart was honored to be chosen, and without needing a title or a name we all became connected. The cost of my fear to first speak up could have cost fully setting them free, but I spoke with faith and honor and the return on that investment has forever changed me and my life.

This I choose to live with as the messages came flying out and serves as a reminder to stand tall and proud as a human in honor of those who died making sure we had the chance to live. Whatever the cost, I choose to serve the soul of myself and God and no longer be a part of the suffering, but a part of the light within and the light we project out. Upon the presence of those who have in previous life's served at the right hand of God and made the ultimate sacrifices, I have come to recognize the only suffering I have endured was of the ego of my freewill and the willingness to prostitute and sell myself off to the lowest bidder for the energy or the life within.

As I look at the cost of those who have made the ultimate sacrifices to place themselves in the line of fire to serve and protect, I think how dare I complain? How dare I continue to suffer when the Healer of Earth and the many who archetype His likeness with such humbleness and suffered in silence, tortured by a society that have yet to understand that they too have suffered for the last time on the cross, but continue to carry the burden of ego of selfishness, judgement, fear, and the highest of all entitlements. The surrender of entitlements will be forever released and replaced with a sense of honor, gratitude and love for what God shall give to me, but first I had to see through the eyes of those who have given their all without the need for a title.

The version of freedom that I had envisioned and read about in the dictionary, now the book of lies in my world, had become so far from the original thought that I found myself questioning my very existence. My days that had become full of blessed opportunities to help heal others, had instead switched to a dread of waking up to the fear of losing the little I had in this human material world. Death, destruction, and dismantling was at my doorstep. What had now become a means of survival, was displayed as outfits on a hanger projecting a representation of myself. A reminder that setting myself free would imprison those I love to a life of suffering, seeing Mediums like me grasp hold of any and all connections to the woman and mother they all once knew. Sadly, it is a truth and yes it was the reality I was living in, but as with every story we tell ourselves, so much of this version was far from the real truth. What it was costing me and what I was yet to let break away from was the sense of worthiness! Who was I to create a life of wealth? I still had an overpowering fear of what all my other businesses and my parent's business had cost them. The humanness of me is reminded that I am a woman who has spiraled into the depths of fear, displayed as my false reality within the illusions and traps of lies.

The illusions of endless abundance had run out in my material world and I found myself at the end of what this dictionary definition of joy and existence would cost me. My truth was that

I was in-between a state of fully leaving my safe job of thirty years as a cosmetologist and stepping full-time into a life as this woman I am today, and yes, I did eventually make it! In reflecting back, my reality was that I had come from a family and a life where I was not taught about finances and we just lived, we just existed. Bad behavior was what it was, much of life was swept under the rug, and we were the perfect picture of a modern-day family. That false picture of having and keeping a family together, I am sure, cost my parents everything.

I left home with a conviction in my heart and a desire to be all that my heart craved, and of course not once was there an awareness as to what I would be teaching and living in this present day. I had no understanding at the time of the importance of fixing the foundation, as that would have been unheard of in my conditioning at that stage, to believe I (we) were fine so just go to school. I left home with no idea or concept of life, and within those pitfalls of life, crumbled and fell into the shadows of all things deemed unacceptable, such as having an affair at twenty-one years of age with a man who showed me attention and told me all the right things a girl with no confidence after years of abuse and being cheating on wanted to hear.

Life just became a series of living in moments of false love with men who were incapable of love, but I chose the broken, running from my jobs just as they were becoming close to being successful. My fear of freedom had become both my enemy and my best friend. My attachment to my lack of worth came from the stories of my mother, and those stories have cost me everything time and time again, as I placed blame and created a "claim to fame" as the "good girl." Meanwhile, I was suffocating the life out of any shred of hope of living a life that was in any way, shape or form close to my true essence. I had perfected putting a false face on for the world, and sadly no one would have ever known. That life, those masks, cost me everything that I could have been. But sitting in that energy again feeds the "shoulda, coulda, woulda" game instead of accepting responsibility for my choices and actions. I made those adult choices and I followed through with the behavior and patterns for many years. Along with the gift of being creative and being a professional caretaker to bad behavior, I crafted a life that would transform and grow, then crumble and fall, and of course every time it was "The money's fault, or the man's fault," and all other scenarios around me, but never mine. Yet, every single time, it cost me dearly, it cost me everything!

Having now arrived at this place of reflecting back on my story, and sitting in a new day, one that lives with the awareness of my Savior's eyes who has lent me His eyes, I have a new perspective, a beautiful new view of all that once was and all that was needed to deflate me, to awaken me. To bring me to a place of seeing that my investment into me has been the best damn investment ever! I have discovered, as I found the courage to look back at my life and acknowledge the expensive payment I made for this front seat view, that my view is now guided by the one thing I am discovering has always been my strongest quality, my faith in the God consciousness. That understanding was a gift and it was given freely. What had the biggest price tag was my faith in myself, understanding that this life of joy and happiness cost me all of who I was, but blessed me with all of who I am about to become.

I have many stories and chapters to go but I want you to know that as this book continues and unfolds back to the beginning of my journey it also arrives at the end of the stories about my pain. To break the cycle, we have to meet back at the beginning to be reborn to live in a truth and not the illusions of the truth. My faith, my love, my loyalty, has no cost, but my worth and value are priceless. If you want to continue the journey from here, I invite you to set that intention for yourself. To know that your life, just as my life, is now in the flow of freedom or in the words of Joel Osteen, "I am now lending and not borrowing." I have a heart that will lend a helping hand, a life I can picture as free of debt and burdens, but also with an acceptance that the human world is simply happening around me, not attacking or taking from me. To be alive I have to feel, but to be free I shall not hide. What I was giving out for free was draining an already empty container and at a cost I am no longer willing to pay. I would wake up to look in the mirror and see that cost staring back at me. The last strand of the "claim to fame" gift of youthful appearance, I had been reminded of many a times that I was blessed to have because of good genetics. Just one more part of my life where another person had claimed an aspect of my greatness. My desire is to tell this story from the point of where I am and not of where I began on the weak foundation. As you can tell this story is very close to my phoenix experience, my awakening.

The moment, the awakening! All of the big expectations and waiting for something spectacular to transpire. To meet and see the golden light of the God consciousness, at the gate of glory and grace. I was awakened with a crashing bang into the realization that this whole journey, everything that I had undertaken, was all about discovering that I was human! The valuable lessons, reaching this level of awareness, was simply to be aware of my human essence. To understand that the role of human was to be embraced, loved, and revered as the greatest accomplishment we will ever do for our spirit.

I could feel my spirit self, laughing a gut full at me, as I came into this realization! How simple would it have been if all the other humans in my life had come to this realization first! Or if I had just received that simple message earlier in the journey. To know that I was here to experience this human experience! However, it was not to become aware of what my eyes would see, or my body to feel, it was about honoring the actual human itself. To learn to care for it, to nurture it, to keep it safe, respect its needs, hold it as it cried, and set it free as need be, just as having a newborn child. Every rebirth was not about getting closer to God, it was about appreciating the ultimate sacrifice that was made for me to be this human. To understand that the God consciousness has a desire for us as humans to just do things better. To ultimately create another world of love inside of the world that was originally created. A world that knew all things existed in love and all things have unlimited potential, just as we do! We spend a lot of time in this world sacrificing ourselves, punishing ourselves and others, and trying to change others into who we know we should be. We naïvely believe in the illusion that we are in a good enough place within ourselves to expect other people to be the best version of themselves in our lives. Today, I set myself free from this illusion, I think!

A bold statement to make from a female human who is yet to know anything. For today I was once again awakened to a new reality of all that shall be. Awaken, but only in this present moment. The challenge to be faced I am sure, is to stay in this present awareness, conscious of all those visited places of self-sabotage and fear, now stored as experiences, and placed on the shelf. Consciously aware that my role of carrying the burdens and suffering of others is not mine to carry. That the burdens and character traits of my shadow self are just simply a glimpse at the shadows, and a reminder to never let the fear override the faith, or the anger and pain to dilute the light and love. As I was always on a mission to achieve enlightenment, I have discovered peace while sitting in the light of the love of God. I was on a mission to be number one, as I fought with the ego to move pass the child who always felt she was number two and that her needs did not matter. I had been taught and well-conditioned in the belief that I was to put my brother's needs before mine, to shush up and never let the truth of emotions ever fall over my lips. From that viewpoint, I searched everywhere and looked through the eyes of everyone, searching desperately for a chance to be seen as number one. I even searched through the eyes of the Holy, thinking that if I just proved myself by taking every course, and becoming "loyal" to the journey of enlightenment and spiritual awakening, that someday I would ascend to the heavens in a light, or I would be sitting in the glow of beautiful robes. Nope, that mindset just created a series of disastrous crash landings, skidding and falling back into the shadows, reaching, and pulling myself up. With determination and a will to not give up, I smiled and chuckled in relief with every moment, or allowed the flow of tears to pour out until there were none left, and the salt stopped stinging my cheek. This reunion was never pretty, and I have never made it to being number one through it all, but I have truly arrived at a place of oneness within my core.

I have come to realize the only one who can truly grant you first place is yourself, ultimately, we are just not that damn special! Sit down, fuse your ego, stop searching so hard for enlightenment, pick up the mirror and take a good look at you! Yes, you! Now understand that just as everyone else has lent you their eyes to look into your soul, you can also take a good look at your own! Look deep! That soul was always just fine. It needed nothing more of you then to provide the human experience, and now are you ready to discover that you are at the place where the opportunity for peace is looking you straight in the eye? This is the reunion of the soul and of a peace that comes with surrendering over the desire to search endlessly for what it has already achieved, enlightenment within.

The soul wanted you to be the one to discover, to overcome the tests and challenges, and remain in the light of love. To be aware that the moments of all that is existing is just temporary to your time upon earth. The soul essence has been waiting to experience the joy and beauty of the God creation through your eyes, for He gave you the eyes and He now wants to use them to see all that is taking place, giving you hints and signs when it's not going as planned, but still allowing you freewill to decide your own truth and live your life. But to return to this soul essence, we must work with and without the faith when the fog appears and challenges us to see in the dark. Without the reunion, the cost may be more than you can afford to pay, and the time traveling blind becomes exhausting. Trust me I know! The cost of my repayment plan is almost complete, but the lessons I feel will be a little less than that place of peace and faith. The cost of full enlightenment is death. That rush to the end or to the front of the line may not be what you had hoped for, but the journey along the way could be everything you dreamed of and your eyes may be blessed with experiences that will fill the soul to a level that it infuses the wattage of the light of the universe.

Can you imagine that the potential effect of a smile, a "Hello," a hug, or an "I love you," could brighten the universal light on such a level that it may possibly break through all barriers of all that exists within the lower vibrations. Keeping in mind that the balance of the experience has to have light and dark, and that the experience will not go without a cost of some pieces of your heart. I do not live on rainbows and unicorns, but I do believe in the magic that all things are possible. I am willing to pay the cost of believing in magic, are you?

CHAPTER 4

The mirror reflection

WHO DOES SHE THINK SHE is? I feel it and hear the whispers of it. It is funny how society likes you the best when you are down. Sadly, I have seen that story so many times as people applaud what they perceive as failure. I have witnessed and heard the whispers of pleasure during moments within my own life when I would tumble and fall.

I think back to the stories I have heard regarding the intentional, well planned takeover of the business that had been providing us life during my childhood, and clearly see the blood, sweat, tears, and all the hopes and dreams. The life savings and everything tied up along with the heart and desire from one man who wished to bring life to a town and give back to its people. To help his hometown grow once again to its glory days of the town it use to be, but this time it was of granite and headstones, ironic to the death I saw in his eyes as I watched him walk down the street empty and depleted after the business was taken over. Sadly, so many cheered as they had believed they were provided a job and a pay cheque but were ultimately making us rich! See the stories we tell ourselves and then convince ourselves that they must be true. The man who is dear to my heart was providing opportunities and taking the lead role of putting himself in the direct line of fire, absorbing both the risk and the cost. The reflection of perceived reality was evident in the eyes of everyone involved in the story, which somehow became tied to worth and value. The story changed from one person to the next, depending on if it was told through the angry lips of resentment, joy filled lips of celebration, or ultimately from the fall or win of those in the takeover position. It all comes back to reflection!

For myself, it was when the door opened, and I saw his presence surrounded by his feelings of defeat, shame, and sadness. My faith in humanity, compassion, and kindness became weaker. Trust? Well that was just contributing to the well stacked up stories of trust issues I had compiled in my head. What was the real truth? Who knows? The stories had become diluted in ego, but the truth I started to trail was a reflection of lack, defeat, and a fear of making it to the top of the empire, a true reflection of settling for comfort. See how we are flung into suffering and the reflection of our shadows. We are conditioned to our realities, our human eyes lie, and all too often we become the reflection of our parent's traumas and stories.

The ah ha moment of realizing you are becoming your parents or stuck in a repeat of their life, and you pause to question, is this my truth? Is this working for me? Even if they were the best Brady bunch family, you are still trying to compare what your eyes have seen. Eventually you find yourself sinking into the reality that there must have been more happening behind the scenes. You start feeling the collapse of the pressures of perfection, and the reflection of everything you rebelled against since you were a kid. For me it was button up blouses and the words, "You will look like a lady and be more presentable." I was not a lady! I was a kid, a teenager. I was the reflection of my mother at that age with a fear of some man invading my personal space because of her stories. My mother was just trying to heal and protect the young girl inside herself through my eyes. This was of course being reflected back to me as, "I am not good enough." Those stories had continued up until this time in my life, and I still to this day, choose by choice, to wear the inappropriate shirts and show off my cleavage, because I am a woman and I like my cleavage. Also, I believe I may have been hung in another life for being a witch but that is for another book. For now I will let the witch in me sit in the reflection of all you are about to read, and I now accept, after years of the stories and years of sabotaging the mind, body, and spirit. You wake up, you are done letting others walk over you, and most of all you are done living on repeat, or allowing life to be sucked from your veins. When the vein of your existence becomes misery, you create the reality you really want to see on social media as a way to lie to yourself, through filtering and editing your images and words.

We look for the perfection and we become done with the picture of perfecting a life that we survived during the days of imperfection, maybe not well, and yes, we have all come through still a little distorted. The true self will take time, but that moment of being done is that turn around moment, just like Bonnie Tyler's song, "Total Eclipse of The Heart." If you are a teenager of the eighties you probably just had a flash back moment as I did! Big Aqua Net hair sprayed hair, unmoving in the wind, turning around with our big eyes of blue and pink flickering back at us. If you are not a teenager of the eighties, well you are missing a moment, but there was the button up loose blouse with the broach, the image of all things "lady like" of the eighties for properly dressed styling teenagers. Mixed mash of Victorian and Rocker Chick all mixed into one. Well that was just a total runaway moment, but it was the beginning of a new time of humans wanting to break free of the conditioning. It was the beginning of our world's expanding, exposed to a much bigger mirror then my Tommy Hunter watching evenings, when the reflection was of wholesome comfort all while sitting with the ultimate reflection of love portrayed by my grandparents and what I still reflect to be a perfect evening, sitting in their love without a word just a smile and comfort. The reflections of safety before I ventured further into my shadow of accomplishing, pleasing, and losing my worth. All of this leads back to the stories of setting the sabotage free and finally waking up. The realization of the harm and punishment I had bestowed upon myself as we all do, in order to be enough, achieve perfection, and to be seen and heard!

I still remember the day I walked up with excitement to greet a client I had been giving my all to for over 10 years, and watched as she stopped, looked at me and said, "Oh you look familiar but where do I know you from?" Yes, I did actually answer. Remember being liked was a priority for me. I answered politely by reminding her of my name and purpose in her life. Her first response was not the one that put a dagger to my heart, but the second one that was to follow. "Oh, I did not know who you were away from your hairdressing chair, I have never seen you anywhere else." I had been invisible in so many ways outside of the role of my life. That moment was a moment of awareness of how invisible I had become. I had sunken into the shadows of my job, my business, my life, my family. I had given my all for so many years helping to perfect the exterior images of women, wanting to stay loved by all, on top of an industry where you only matter based on the quality of the work you perform that day. Putting on the mask and the face to be present, became my life as I watched myself decay and fall further and further away from the center of my soul and from my light.

I awakened one day to the reminder of my light and I had to ask myself, "Where did you go?" I had to look in the mirror, look at the hundred plus extra pounds of protection and armor and the sluggish skin with saggy, sad eyes and say, "I see you!" This was the day I awoke to the reminder of my lack of worth. I had been conditioned to believe that giving up my needs was expected. I stopped seeing the star in waiting and gave my light to anyone who just looked into my eyes. Then comes the day you stop! You look in that mirror and say, "You deserve it all."

I often get asked by the elderly, or see the look of dislike, that I have learned to not take it personally, as I hear the whispers of, "Who does she think she is?" For the first time in my life l can honestly answer that today I do know who I am! I had a story in my head for too many years to count. A story of sadness and of a mirror image of a puppet on a string, that as I think of in this moment makes me chuckle at the ridiculous thought of mind control, but also with a sadness of the impressionable impact that society, perspective, and words can have on a child's mind.

My sensitive soul and already tainted spirit from the insecurities of a mother with image issues that I could not understand with compassion until this stage of the game, was reminded of a mental relationship I carried of an image of a pig, along with a story of pain from being teased by youth who had a desire to laugh at everything. I found myself in a moment when, I thought I was on my way through the golden gates of awareness, but the image of the pig once again resurfaced in my human eyes and the annoying nagging voice rang in my ears. I found myself quickly going to my story of pain as the many memories of rolling names surfaced of being called annoying, ugly, and overweight. Images of characters representing these names came flooding back, stemming from the mouth of the youth in my life who were simply just full of imagination, a sense of humor mixed I am assuming, with their own hurt. As I started repeating to my partner and a friend the story of being called "Miss Piggy," who I had portrayed as fat and annoying, I found myself glancing back at the TV and with a chuckle, a smile, and then a laugh, as I realized that I had long since moved beyond the pain of the name. I was once again seeing the reflection as Miss Piggy appeared on screen! "Oh my," I chuckled, "I am a little like Miss Piggy! Eyelashes, cleavage and larger than life!" My view has changed, and I now see Miss Piggy as a beautiful, confident woman, beating to her own drum, demanding that her needs be met, and insisting that she is to be valued. Hell, she even had red shoes, a signature true to my style! She was a woman of empowerment, that sadly I could not see until my 48-year-old self had finally removed the shadow from the mirror to see the truth of a pig.

As I peel back the layers of myself and the days changed, my eyes now reflect a woman of empowerment and strength. Tomorrow I will get to know another new version of her, and I will embrace her a little more compassionately than the day before. I am a woman of strength who, for the longest time put too much focus into making sure all was well for everyone else, but I have since awakened to a feeling in my heart that I was finally free. Free of what, I did not know at that moment, until I walked past my mirror that is half covered by a TV and another quarter covered by my pile of jewelry. I could see through to the last corner left and for the first time in months I heard, "Wipe the dust off."

The dust of sprays and perfume residues that were masking myself once again, but this time it was not out of fear but out of survival. To survive the journey, I had to endure to walk the underworld of my past choices and release the life I have so desperately clung onto, a life of what use to be magic and pain all in one. The magic was the creation of a business I watched grow and crumble as the facade of artificial exterior happiness could not be upheld, but the blessing of finding all of my broken beautiful self inside of a world that drew in all that needed a place to call home. Home in a world built inside of a box. I had to feel the pain of crucifying myself one last time so that when I dusted off that mirror, I was dusting it for the very last time. The clarity of my life, the self-loathing and desire to find outside love in those more broken than I could have ever been, had finally come to an end.

I am dusting off the mirror for one last time as I finally feel my way through the pain in my heart and into the beauty of the scarred life I am blessed to now live in love. The reflection of pain has become the reflection of the awakened. The butterfly or Miss Piggy, whichever I am transforming into love, turned inward, and a reflection that reflects outward. There comes a time when understanding that when you pray every day for God to take you out of the pain, you stop looking in the mirror with clarity. We stop seeing that it has become dusty and murky, until the day God awakens you and asks, "Have you shown yourself enough of the hell, are you ready?"

Today as I write this truth, Jesus has taken the wheel and those in the spirit world have taught me the truth of faith. As I spent weeks looking at bottles of liquid that could take me to peace, I had made a choice to walk in the shadow of the pain and illusion of the stories, carrying the pain of those who have walked before me. But today, I awakened to dust the mirror. Today I saw the truth beyond the veil, and found a faith in the valley with peace, hope, and the power within the Divine. I am, you are, we are all the reflection of the Divine. Our pain is in the details of our stories, our happiness is the creative beauty, and the scars are the push of strength we look towards others to bring us.

As we go inward, we finally become ready to look with the eyes of truth at the beauty that comes when we dust off the mirror. If today you cannot dust off your mirror, I ask of you to have the courage to ask someone who has dusted theirs, to hold the space as you walk through the pain of your underworld until the day you can dust off your own mirror. Let us be the reflection of love and hope, not the reminder of fear and failure. Are you ready to dust off your mirror?

CHAPTER 5

The not so pretty process

THROUGH THE EYES OF THE God consciousness we are all beautiful. Yes, that is hard to see but you have to look beyond the human to see that the beauty was hidden as early back as the newborn child. A child born to a mother who has not experienced love, safety, or security. Has never been taught to nurture her soul, becomes a mother who carries her fears of mothering over to a newborn child and the not so pretty process of projections begin again and the cycle continues! That is where we need to go to be able to forgive. Forgive but not forget, has been a place I could stand on my soap box and speak a truth I dare not speak for way too long. I can tell you so much of what I have lived was not so pretty, but it was a creation of someone I see as so beautiful when I look in the mirror.

I think through the eyes of having lived those moments, to the times of where my beautiful presence was intimidating enough to lash out to or to feed her without even knowing she shrunk away from her own beauty and allowed herself to be shadowed. It has taken me a lot of years to be at this point and place in my life. We should never be a bother, but we should always be a part of the beauty of the process, as an opportunity to explore and discover that beauty through the eyes of others, learning to except that not all who enter into your life will come with good intentions. Whether conscious or not, the shadows and darkness of the intentions exist and there is often a point where you will convince yourself that you were to blame, that you were not worthy, and this is the beauty of the process. What strength it takes to be taken to that place of awareness and still rise above it. The process allows us to look deep within, to see all the character roles we play, including the villain, because we all have monster moments! I know I am about to hear a few, "Oh not me I would never be that way." I can tell you with absolute certainty that, "Yes you can. We all can!" In level two of the *More Than Existing* coaching program called, *Existing Beyond The Reflection,* we learn to get real with our shadow, so that before we all start kicking it around, we really take the time to listen to her/him, acknowledging the roll our shadow self plays. What was that ugly saying again? Are we protecting our shadow or reaching out for it?

I remember this day so clearly and oh how proud I was at myself for my crazy ass moment. My daughter was 14, had her learners license and wanted to drive. First came the moment of guilt, as I realized I was teaching my daughter to tell a little white lie, as I told her not to tell her father that I let her drive our truck, which I was paying half for. An invasion of fear and my master moment of not so pretty behaviors, as I was defying and lying.

This chapter may be one of the hardest for me to write. The beauty I have within me I spent so many years trying to take away, to downplay so that others would become more comfortable. I made the bad behaviors of others acceptable and became a victim to the addiction of smoothing over the anger, all of which I am fully aware of. This behavior was fully learned from the conditioning of a mother who made the behavior of my sibling something we all had to accept. Not just accept, but give into it for the moment of peace that could be obtained if we all just gave in. I was taught to just "ignore" a powerful word that inflates the spaces within the mind of a child, and later inflates the ego of the narcissist tendencies of the men to follow.

My mother unintentionally taught me to ignore the flags, to just be quiet and contribute to the silent conversation. That suppression became compiled in the head of a voiceless child who then turned into a voiceless and powerless woman. This is not a "blame your mother" or "blame another" game, it's the truth of the not so pretty mess of stories that are built from what our eyes see, our ears hear, and our hearts hold. The beautiful creation of a perfect storm! Behind the scenes, I am sure, was a mother who did not know what to do with the busy, hyper energy, and a sensitive daughter within her house every day. All of this would have certainly taken its toll on a young mother in her twenties who had not learned the best of mothering from her own mother. We see the uglies of so many families and we wonder why the empires tumble and fall. Well, sometimes there is just not enough of a foundation to hide the imperfections of pain.

I am not going to lie, there are days when I want to go back to the anger, but I have learned to truly embrace the beauty of my shadow, and understand that I could not fully separate from all of the shadows, otherwise how then would I know joy, if I did not know pain? How would I know my happiness without some experiences of sadness? And trust me, as with all of us, there were some experiences we could have done without! When you turn your contempt to an inward perspective it becomes shame, and so begins the game that takes us the furthest from our light and out of the beauty of seeing the moments of grace.

No one ever said falling apart was pretty and I can confess that I have had some real ugly moments. I had to get fucking angry before I could turn to the shame, look it in the eyes with the mirror in front of me, and see the beautiful reflection that had become hidden so far away from the origin of the light within! I have spent a lifetime tidying up, hiding, and saying that it is okay! It is okay that you placed me as second, or less than in your life, or that I made it acceptable to do so to myself, in my own life. My essence of love was never inside of me, so how could I ever expect anyone to bring their love into me and share that love? Instead my love was so far on the outside of me that I appeared to be selfish, but my truth is that I have been living a life of desperation and despair. The only reflection I could see was the not so pretty defeated self that had been glaring back at me with anger and disgust.

My love had been so far out there that my relationships became a desperation for me to give all of my everything to just be enough for once in my life. To find that one person who could truly become loyal to me, but how was that ever to be possible when I have always been cheating on my own heart. Prostituting it out as if I might as well sell it to the undeserving. "Why not sell it short?" My shadow voice would say as I continued to hear in the unspoken words and actions of those around me that I am not worthy of the golden treatment and respect that I imagine they give to those from the infused love I have injected into their hearts, as I poured all of mine into theirs, I guess as I was conditioned to do. As I cleaned the spaces on the outside of me, I was continuing to carry the dirty secrets of shame within.

I had lots of space in the basement of my empire, of myself, and had allowed others to dump their garbage into me. I was not filling this empty space with my own desires of what it takes to house love on the inside. Looking back, it was such cluttered mess and confusion, no wonder I questioned my identity. If your reflection outward has become ugly, it is time to look at the ugly truth on the inside.

I had found myself slowly moving into the actual basement of the house, feeling that this home was never truly mine. In this space, I found myself creating a beautiful comfortable place with the one red chair which would become my hug of comfort as I became aware of the reflection in all the eyes around me, mirroring a reflection of who I had become. I cannot tell you the exact day of my awakening to the personal misery I had trapped myself in, but I clearly remember the day that the cord snapped. It was the day I could bend metal and what should have been almost impossible was so easy to do, and in that moment, I truly learned the powerful energy behind our words. This story has a life of its own, but it became the power of projection to the statement of chapter one. I knew in that moment I was done with all the persecution, judgements, and shaming I had experienced in the not so pretty process, and in that moment, I knew there was no going back.

That moment I walked to the basement and with tears in my eyes I sat on my single person red chair and wrote.

"Today I am done, and I am about to find a life of joy and happiness, no matter the cost." What did I have to lose? Sacrificing my light had already cost me everything. Through the eyes of those looking in, I had everything in the material world, but I had become an empty shell that was caused by a lifetime of believing I was here to carry the pain and suffering of the world. Living in traumas that sometimes were not mine, conditioned to the unhealthy trauma responses of some of the adults in my life, and carried them forward as if they were true to me. Topped with my own trauma and doing everything I could to be a better mother than my mother. The stories we create and live become the not so pretty mess that overshadows the remembrance of all the beautiful experiences that had also followed us through. My mission in self-discovery was to start by remembering the beautiful moments and people in my life, remembering the beautiful experiences with the people who had lent me their eyes to see.

I can guarantee you it may not be the most beautiful experience but it is worth what it will cost you and the return on your investment contributes to the strength in the foundation you have been building from the time we started this journey of being a human. Are you ready to start your process? Do you have a desire screaming from the inside out that this is the time to choose to start creating your beautiful experience?

CHAPTER 6

The impossible fork to bend

"I AM DONE," HAD BEEN silently echoing in my head for many years, but it was just a whisper. It was in the silent breeze and moments of peace, when I would sit on the little dock in a campground that for years became my escape from the reality of the life I was living of my own accord, making a choice to suffer my own punishments of pain for the choices I had made in the past.

As I sat my heavy, achy body down, I would look out over the swampy waters and look at all the beauty that had found a life within the murky water, realizing that the water was trapped in the confinements of the walls that contained it. I would speak to the animals of their brilliance for choosing to find safety in the comforts of the well-hidden murky waters. Waters, that had truly created a whole ecosystem of its own and was well providing for the needs of all those who chose to live there.

In the stillness of a silent breeze, I had a thought and image of "This is how so many of us are living. This is how I was living, trapped in a murky life that had become a comfort to my pain, providing all that I had convinced myself I needed." I had become trapped in the system. I could see the life existing

35

and what my human eyes were seeing was the story I told. I had become the victim to my circumstances and had started to become comfortable in what I was starting to believe was to be all of my existence, until the day I decided to buy a kayak. I think back now to that single purchase, having chosen the color yellow, the color of our power center. The universe is funny that way. To top it all off, the animals I would watch were mainly beavers as I enjoyed watching them build an empire, living within the false reality of their safety.

I bravely and single handedly, loaded the kayak into my truck, drove to the swamp and placed it in the water, proud of my accomplishment. Then came the fear that was originally not on my radar, as I tried to figure out how to get my large body into the small opening. I felt like an octopus squeezing into a bottle, and the fears of being laughed at and teased as a child came flooding back in, but I did it! Once that challenge was achieved, in rushed the next thought, "How would I get out?" I would obsess about this in my cluttered brain, a mixture of faith and disaster.

I kayaked the swamp waters, exploring and learning to maneuver the paddles, and relaxed as I started to become the captain of my journey into new lands. It was a start to the adventures of my own stories within my head until my dearest friend joined in a little blue kayak, so appropriate to the voice she needed to find. Like a little sister would do she followed along. Together, but alone, we braved the waters of the deep dark sea of a small little swamp that we had claimed as our home away from home. Together, we have a bond of love that we spent a lifetime seeking, and a true test of trust in the ability to adapt to our ever-changing lives. Find the friends who have faith and believe in something that will hold you steady. Soulmates of loving relationships come in many forms resembling a fork we might bend but would never break.

Together, we eventually ventured beyond the confides of the swamp, out into the flowing, clear, fresh water. With every adventure, I stuffed my body into the kayak and promised myself that this too shall change. I knew in my heart, that just as I broke free of the swamp water, situations within the confinements of my life would also begin to change. I discovered that the beavers I once believed lived happily in their sanctuary of muddy peace and were content within a confined home, actually enjoyed a whole intricate underground system that flowed back and forth between both worlds. With shock and amazement that my stories of reality had once again changed, I was aware of the lies my human eyes could tell. Now aware of the freedom I could create without leaving my comfort zone, I began to dig my way out and start a new life.

My illusion of being trapped was only in my head. The push and desire to camp and kayak all changed after a series of unfortunate and sad events mixed in with a desire to move beyond the confinements of my small town. The breaking point was the day I went back to check on the beavers, only to discover their home had been destroyed. An anger grew inside of me and my heart exploded with a truth that our existence had to be built on a strong foundation, which could sustain a life no one else could take, as it could only be built on the inside. Life looked, felt, and became different from that moment, and within the comforts of my basement I found a solution to lose the weight and set myself free from my own entrapment. The tools of healing I had, the faith in me I had to find, and the courage was building but not yet all the way there.

Everything passed by so quickly and within a few years I found myself stretched out on a surgical table with a smile on my face, as I was aware that what I needed to succeed in my weight loss journey would require assistance from a surgeon. With no regrets, I happily took the journey into a new human shell that went through many changes and processes, but that is another story for another book.

My mirror reflection had been changing and my smile grew,

but I was not giving myself time to heal and adjust, which later would become part of the emotional problems I would have to face. This leads me to the journey of bending a fork, one of many things that I thought would be impossible to do, but as I was discovering, my realities and truths were bending and shaping on a regular bases, synchronicity was in play everywhere.

While still recovering from gastric bypass surgery, I attended The Speak, Write and Promote, Hay House Event in Scottsdale, Arizona and while eating lunch watched a woman who was also attending, take a single fork and bend it with her mind while speaking about the power of thoughts. The books written by Louise Hay and Dr. Wayne Dryer, were the bibles of my soul, but that day it finally clicked! My way out was in a fork! With a desire in my heart and a still cluttered mind, I missed the deadline of entry for the Hay House Speak, Write and Promote Event, but I now had a fork. Daily, I would try to bend the fork as I spoke my words of truth, "I am worthy." Nothing. I knew I was not believing my own words. I was so good at helping others but in believing my own worth and speaking of its truth, I was definitely failing myself. Like the beavers who stayed so committed to their journey and mission, I would also have to commit to accepting and believing my worth.

Then came the day when the words of criticism placed upon my life, would finally cause me to declare, "I AM DONE!" With that the fork bent and I knew something was about to change. I proudly went back to the basement, placed my fork where I could see it, and started to tell everyone so I could hold onto the moment and believe in the power of my words and thoughts.

I remember the moment I showed my daughter my bent fork and spoke of how impossible it had been to bend until I spoke a truth that I still did not say out loud. She was in awe and so interested to hear of my story. Speaking my truth, filled the room with a silence and disbelief, and as we all parted ways, I looked into my daughter's eyes witnessing her sadness for me in that moment. Those eyes spoke volumes, and no words needed to be said. Within weeks I found the courage to speak a truth that was long overdue and made the decision to leave a relationship that I am thankful for experiencing. Learning to see your reflection through the eyes of another, allows forgiveness to transpire easier than you may think. Through those reflections I saw my pain and the desire to fix others was really a desire to repair myself, a truth I was not ready to see before.

In the end, I was free and that impossible fork to bend became a true representation of the power of projection to get to where I am today. Bending forks never became part of my practice as I knew folding was about bringing my attention inward, becoming focused on what was needed to move forward, and a true reminder of the strength within. Today you may feel trapped in a place of judge and jury. Take the time to explore, and then reach out for that right person to hold space as you take the steps to move beyond the confinements of your walls. You may not know your strength but today get that fork and place it in your hands and make sure its strong and heavy and not the one that can be easily bent. The journey may seem impossible somedays but with an unbendable faith and a commitment to keep on trying, there will be a day when it will bend, and all reality will bend with you.

CHAPTER 7

Finding the faith

GOD NEVER PREPARED US FOR the heartbreak and pain that would be upon us, we were not prepared to be humans. We were shown the light as we arrived as a reminder to trigger our awakening from the forty weeks in the dark, and were shown the beauty of love through another human's touch. The rebirth begins every day as we awaken from the darkness of sleep and are shown the beauty of the sun, reminding us that every day the sun will rise, and the sun will set, for every day is a rebirth, a new opportunity. Some days will shine bright and others it will hide behind the clouds. There will be days that the storms will have to appear as sadly that's a part of the process and not a question of, "Why me?"

There will always be a time when each and every one of us will have to endure the storms. I used to say, "Be thankful you have another day," but that statement became harder to make as I spent many years behind the chair as a hairdresser, made many friends, and saw many go through losses that are unbearable to the soul. My work as a medium and healer has taken me to a place where my faith in humans and the human experience has been questioned time and time again. My truth is, I have no answers, and I do not preach faith to those with stories I cannot explain. All I know is I am a spiritual healer who guides through holding space with love and compassion. An open channel from the moment I am asked to bring the messages of love as a reminder of the powerful eternal light of those we hold dear to our hearts. The grief never ends, but the process changes. "Live for those who did not get to live," is the message that echoes loud, as my dear child is the light that has infused my heart with more love than I can contain within me, as with all the other children and loved ones of the spirit world. Today I can tell you the call to love and the mission of so many, is to be the voice of strength, courage, and to hold space for those not yet strong enough to hold their own. Faith is a kindness and compassion without words or questions!

I understand and yet do not understand the stories of our contracts. Why would I have contracted to meet my child and to then choose to not allow him to come to a full life? I myself have questioned many times, the process that unfolds as we have to endure the human journey. Yes, after all these years I have questions where I still seek the answers.

All I know is the truth of my story and experience, as I moved past the illusions of reality and reminded my barely breathing self of the faith that God has had in me. A faith that finally took me to understand "grace" as I stood in front of an image of Mother Mary and Jesus and was asked to have faith in the process. The process of being the humble messenger of reuniting the souls of the beautiful spirits that have been waiting in the light, for the mothers and fathers to walk from their shadows and feel the essence of a love that is eternal. From faith, I can now speak the truth of my true self, as I have built a loving relationship with all versions of my shadowed self. I was afraid, I felt alone, and I was a pleaser conditioned in the trauma of choosing to make another's life more important than my own or my child's. As I sit in the forever story of my role in the loss of my child, my faith in the internal light of the spirit is always present within the heart of a grieving human soul. When we are strong enough to look through the eyes of our own God conscious soul, we return to the faith that our loved ones are ever present. A return to my faith after many years of nailing myself to crosses, carrying a whip and whipping myself with words and actions of shame, I have been taken to a place of looking closely through my own eyes at the soul. I have walked many journeys with the dark souls, and I have come to the awakening moment of truth that the light was always guiding me to a point where the freewill process was to reach out and up, or stay looking down and into the darkness of my pain. I reached out and up, and faith is why I now have the strength to speak my truth.

My story has a light and a darkness, as does the day and the night, it never goes without question whether another will appear again. There is a faith in the process of Mother Earth and the matrix that we are only now awakening to, it starts with love and is fueled by faith. As with my story, I am not for or against anything, I am in support of awareness, knowledge, and a choice to decide what aligns to your soul.

I had to heal, and this would take revisiting all of my past, stopping along the way to all the places of grief, disappointment, hurt, and pain, to see the worth that just had not been there. To the voice that had been hushed up and the conditioning that moves us to our biggest faith of all, the faith within.

I had asked to be returned to the vision of the days and all that had transpired, to the words prior, and truth no one had heard. Fear was what was at play for myself, for I cannot speak for a father whose story is not in any way mine to tell. But I can speak of the fear in the heart of a single mom, who had one little girl who needed a mom, with a cup that was too full to care for her. The anger that was alive and a message from a doctor of the possible problems that she believed were transpiring once again, removed me from my faith in myself and my abilities, and took me to a decision that I realize now had become the projection of a life of learning my worth, my value, and powerful faith I doubted within. The moment of "no" had been a moment too late and so the journey to suffer on the cross of persecution would begin. I carried a guilt in my heart as I witnessed each of my friends crumble in a pain that there were no words to explain, and added in the guilt of the healer in me that would have to sit helplessly by, to be just a friend on those days.

In my own code of ethics and integrity, I sit as a human friend before anything, with compassion until the day I am asked to be of service. There are no messages that can repair a heart that is forever broken. There is just over time a golden light that infuses the wound with unconditional love and a former bond of strength that we had no idea was possible. This has been a truth of the human journey, and testimony of my faith in the works of the divine timing, and not the ego's desire to "fix" what cannot be repaired.

What I know in my heart and soul, is that my unborn child appears and speaks to me as my son, and in my healing journey has been named Joshua. Now a guide to my faith, and yes I carried a guilt in my heart as I witnessed each of my friends crumble in a pain that there are no words to describe, but I have set myself free of my own punishment. Moving past my selfish desire to punish myself, I became as selfless as humanly possible to the service of my spiritual duty, and through the eyes of those in pain now send loving prayers of strength, and ask to hold the eternal light of a flame we cannot see without faith that there is always light in the dark.

I am reminded daily we cannot have light without darkness, but the sun will rise again. As I sleep in the darkness, asking in my prayers to be strengthened in faith and for the love in our hearts to be ever reaching out in service to those who cannot see. When I awake, I ask again in my prayers to bless me to have only the healthy ego of confidence and strength, to remember to be thankful for the opportunity to be awake and fully embrace the human experience if even just for one more moment. For Mother Theresa has taught me, through our many moments of channeled messages, that one more moment of changing myself can be a part of the movement to change the world. Be kind to yourself during the darkness and you will awaken to the light. My duty to my Joshua has been to help the children of the world, and it took me a while to understand that we are all children to the light, including myself. It is a duty that is still unfolding, awakening, and breathing a life of its own. Through my story and many others, I have discovered Mother Theresa has moved past her human judgement upon us, and has become a light at the table of my council of those who knew human conditioned faith, but now understand the power of the faith of the Divine, this is as told to me.

Of all things, whether we agree or disagree, we are reminded to be a light and not an intentional storm in someone's life. It takes enough strength and courage to just get through the fated storms we are unprepared for. Find the strength to reach out, before spewing the storm waters into the hearts of another, and never be afraid to ask to take cover within another's space, without taking over. For the short time we are here on earth, be the ray that brightens someone's day, become the warmth and softness, remember we are all perfectly imperfect, and all a child of the light, these are the moments of living in grace.

CHAPTER 8

The ultimate level of forgiveness

AS I SIT TO WRITE this chapter, I feel my body start to tremor with real human anxiety, and not my spiritual hits when there are messages to convey. This chapter came with some real human truths I would have to face. A reality of humankind and the shadows of not just myself, but others that had been attached to my heart, taking me to that unaware place of giving up my power, and now readiness to start the journey of its return.

I have learned forgiveness on a holy level with Jesus, and that would become so much easier than this would become. I realized I had not been so forgiving of myself and that has been hard to face. I have learned that forgiveness would become the real, raw moments of mercy. The place of realization that I had tried to sell my soul essence to the highest bidder of a soul who walked their own shame, and all because the inner child in me was unaware of the origin of the pain that would lead to adult sabotage. The truth is that forgiving ourselves will be the hardest person we can forgive. The desire to take ownership of pain has been engrained so deeply that it is hard to step away. Through my journey of owning my Goddess and the Witch I appear to be, I have come to the understanding that we have always been feared back into

45

the darkness, because of the not yet awakened still with fears and desires of human control.

The woman I am today can tell you it may have taken almost forty-nine years this time around, and countless life times before, to stand in my light, and not be afraid to walk in the light of forgiveness for myself first, and then in others who have tried to shadow my light. I am sure there will be many more, but I do not fear those who live in the dark, for they are the faceless shadows of myself and my awareness and I have met the ones with no identity before. I am reminded that these are not strangers, but simply an awareness to all that it has taken to return to my light. Speaking your truth after forgiveness, from a place of mercy and love, instead of hate, is a level of vulnerability that is unfolding before my eyes as I write.

My hope is for you to understand the often misunderstood person I have always been. I am a person who can slip easily between worlds perfecting the art of hiding my human self, and allowing my channel to receive the exposure and the voice. This becomes evident in the writings, as you will discover there are separate elements of the human Corrie, and the Divine channel who has an awareness of love and light. My human self, living on the human plain, is still a woman who may slip over to the angry side, have moments of crazy, and experience irrational (but rational to me) moments of explosive expressions of real internal struggles. I can tell you from right here in this place of forgiveness, there is no big beautiful, "ah ha" moment of lights accompanied by the appearance of Angel's singing.

From this place of awareness, I have learned to stop the perfectionist from perfecting, perfectionism. This book and journey you will take with me, read from me, and messages channeled through me, is not perfect. Striving to do the best that I can possibly give that day, and sometimes having nothing. Those days become me days, and this I shall honor. This is my reward in forgiving myself, and the benefit that others receive is through getting the best of me, but also in being reminded that I am just another human, doing the best that I can. Maybe today is your day to reflect on the times you said, "I'm sorry," when you did not mean it, but felt obligated? What if you spewed your shit onto someone else today because you neglected to honor yourself in having a timeout day? I can tell you that I have been there, and yes, I have picked up the phone or sent messages in that moment, that I had no right to deliver and lay my struggles onto them. Why? Because I know what it is like to have had it done onto me, and that takes us back to the shadows we have worked too hard to get out of. "I am sorry," are sacred words and must be given value and not be just words. The biggest mask of fear, the illusion of a reality that no matter the level of pain I am experiencing, I will be okay. No! We are not always okay, and no matter how enlightened you become, you are human and there will be times you are not okay, and that is absolutely okay! Got it! Now remember it when you go to judge yourself or someone else who is having a moment and is on their knees.

I have made a big part of my work about healing emotional wounds and trauma, and as I had to work through healing the physical body, I found myself training over the years in past life healing, studying the amazing energy healing work of Deborah King, and recently mastering somatic training, as it works on the trauma held within the body. Searching for knowledge and wisdom, and not always of this human realm, is a quest that I will forever undertake. The universe has such a way of making us believe that the work we undertake is for someone else and not ourselves, but the reality is that in every session I do, the same healing flows through me, as I am just the vessel.

Having started the second class within the somatic training, something stirred within me that I know sub-consciously to have always known, but didn't want to face, so had hidden it until I was truly ready as a healer to acknowledge, but who really knows? I have learned for the most part we know nothing, just stories.

What I did know was the pain, and it was a very familiar feeling of an invasion upon my soul and upon the feminine within. I had laid a claim that I was never a victim, and as I started to see a little child whose face became mine, I quickly became aware that I had indeed been victimized. How many times in my life had I been a victim but had let it go as if I was not worthy enough of respect. The tears flowed, and I fell to my knees with a desire to support others who clearly had also been the reflection of the child in me. How far back and by whom, I had no desire to know or ever know. What I had become aware of was a truth of a voiceless little girl who everyone said was shy, but she was not shy, she was shadowed.

The story of my life that I am still witnessing, is to not bring up the past and shame those who speak out instead of dealing with a truth of the story deeper at the root. What made these people monsters? At one point they were also children and somewhere along the line someone shadowed their truth, contributing to a world of voiceless victims that would grow and be driven back into the shadows. This became my story of an awareness of what is happening in the human world, but conditioned to turn a blind eye, in fear of facing a reality that would be too painful.

I was three years old. I was wearing pajamas with a print, and there was a man and he somehow inappropriately touched me. I told no one! It was a memory that would appear in all my healing sessions with my dear friend, fellow healer, and social worker. I believe the little girl in me knew she was in a safe place, but the conditioning was still too powerful of a shadow, and I believed in a story that there was no way it could have happened to me, because I had convinced myself that I had a very overprotective mother. She made us wear hats in July to ensure we didn't get ear infections, and tethered (please remember, this was back in the 70's) us to the clothesline so we would stay safe playing outdoors. These were some of her many attempts to protect her children as she was never protected herself.

Every time I mentioned to my mom that this memory was coming up in sessions, she would say it is not possible because she never left us alone, but she did! She always went out, but conditioned me to dismiss what was my truth, and in doing so made the bad behavior of others my pain to wear. I remember that is when I started to go inward, and decided to make it OK for people to mistreat me, cheat on me, and abuse me. Later on, in my adult years, my ribs hurt, and I could not breathe as this story came up. However much I had been disrespected, I kept saying, "It's okay", because their spirit is still a good person. I had been hiding behind my natural strength and gifts, in masking the pain by always being the pleaser in relationships and work.

I had to spend time with the little girl in me. I saw her at an early age when she started to write, until her sibling stole her diary and read it to all the friends in the house. My early childhood family life has given me many great stories, for many books and many years to come. We have a love/hate relationship as kids with those in our lives who are dear to our hearts, but can sometimes feel so far apart from, and there were many moments that I can now chuckle and cry at within my childhood home. All stories I can no longer hide, because life has trapped me to this house, to face my truth of the pain and reality, so that I can finally see the little girl in me and heal. I know this story is not as severe as many others have had to endure, including those within my close inner circle, but it had been the story of the little girl in me who was still trying to protect the adult I had become today, and it was my truth to face.

The day I set her free, and really truly forgave her, was the day I forgave the man responsible for the action, but I will always remember now and will not forget! I did not need to dig further and dig up bones, for the shadow in them no longer was the shadow on me. The inner child in me has now been seen and given a voice! I forgave her forever feeling responsible, and ever feeling the need to make the bad behaviors of others acceptable.

Most of all, I have learned that to forgive is not easy and it needs time. Forgiveness is not for that person who hurt or betrayed you, it is for you, and for you to set yourself free. Your freedom becomes one more step in the ultimate level of *More Than Existing - Living Your Truth!*

It is not okay to be intentionally hurt, and if we unintentionally hurt someone even with our words, take action and say, "I am sorry." It is not okay to be told to hide your pain! Forgiveness for me, is freedom to a voice I was afraid to use, as I used to hide behind my mother's legs, I now know that I had been hiding behind not just my shadow, but my channel as the spiritual world was always my safe place to hide. Going inward was my comfort zone, for living a life of an introvert/extrovert. Because I love, and because I am who God has created me to be, I will always have to be the weird one out there. But, as I grow and heal my circle of those who have forgiven, accepted, and fell in love with me, is now ever expanding.

I now find myself in a place of choosing to place the act of forgiveness in all relationships that have been in my life. Some are much easier than others, and yes there are some I am just not ready to play nice with yet, as the Dixie Chicks song plays in my head, "I am still mad as hell, and I am not ready to play nice." No one can tell us when or how, but remember, the act of forgiveness towards others is the ultimate gift of freedom to yourself!

I have a rebel child in me, and I called her, "My bad child syndrome." She wore a protection of, "I don't care," but she does care, and her battle ridden body full of feeling cares. I now know that I am valuable and worthy of the ultimate gifts. Those whom I have held captive to my pain, or have held me captive to tears, I now set free and break myself free.

Letting go of the emotions of hate and anger, will eventually be replaced with love, compassion, and kindness. Emotions that have held a place in my heart for so long, now have ownership of my whole essence. There were moments I fought with every breath to hold on to all emotions, thinking it was mine to carry. But now, I use all the tools learned over the years, to breathe it out and remember, "I am golden." I am, as we all are, worthy of the golden breath of remembering who we truly are.

There had been an invasion, complete with viruses and contamination, for the lack of self-worth and disrespect of understanding the meaning of loyalty. I had been raped, and stripped down, with words and actions that for a long time destroyed me to my very core, and yet, I still forgave and stood tall. I am a Goddess, with the courage to go the distance because of discovering that I am not here to live in the shadows, I am worthy to live a life of *More Than Existing*.

I had started a process of forgiveness that would take me from the trauma resource of protection, denial, projection of false angry confidence, and into a reality of the lies I lived to protect my truth. For that I forgave myself and vowed to catch myself from this moment forward in my own lies. We create and tell ourselves the stories of this life that we feel suit us during the times of change, reality checks, and decision-making moments. When the reality is that life had stopped me in my tracks to give my human a humbling experience, and reminder of how much strength it would take to get through this life, along with all that it would teach me. I may be the spiritual teacher, coach, and guide to so many, but I will always have moments that will drop me to my knees. As I write, I am there in one of those moments of having to hold my shit together during the day and then crumbling at night as I await answers to many questions that have now changed my life. Hearing, "I am sorry," from the mouth of others, may never fully come. I do not place expectations upon others to be in a place they are not ready to be, and I do not allow it to stop me from forgiving on a level I did not even know possible until now. Why me? Well why not me? It has to be someone and we will all have those difficult moments sadly. The difference is that enough strong voices saying, "Sorry, not today fucker!" May be enough over time to be the change. Yes, that is from the voice of Corrie, and not the beautiful channel who also has no problem dropping an "F" bomb in just the right place.

What have I learned? I will never again intentionally give away the beautiful pieces of myself that I have worked so hard to find. I will value my treasures and gifts and give to all but my most precious of gifts, as these are the valuable treasures that I do not have to give to all.

Sometimes we do not recognize that the emotions of anger and filtered stories of those who love and care for us, are pushed away in moments of disagreement, argument, or out of fear of being hurt. Most of the time these situations could simply be fixed with an, "I'm sorry," or "I forgive you." Reality is that those same people and what put you together in the first place is a common story. A mirror reflection of the internal struggle of jealousy and judgement we subconsciously have when we choose to let the fear of the unknown hold us back while others make the choice to leap towards joy and happiness. The real emotion is often the awareness that our fears and trauma have held us back from truly living. Release the attachment to fear, forgive, and take a good look at what has brought you together in the first place. Remember, that piece is still there inside both of you.

I truly love even those who have turned their backs on me. I forgive the harsh words for they made me stronger and gave me the strength I needed to dig deep, for in forgiving others I learned to forgive myself. I believe we are here to dance, and my leaving this earth song will be Garth Brooks, "The Dance." Living a life of *More Than Existing* has taken me to realize that I may have experienced all of this, but the moments of joy were still there along the way. I forgive myself for ever letting those moments slip away or forgetting to remind another of them before it was too late. Today, forgive yourself and remember to dance.

If I were to leave this earth tomorrow, I can now say I have danced! I have created a transformational, empowerment, and self-actualization coaching program from my life's journey and turned it into the fuel needed to project me further. Never let burdens hold you back! Always remember to dance! Love those that are easy to love less, and most of all love the unlovable more, and just maybe they too will once again dance!

CHAPTER 9

The realness of the reality is that we all lie

I HAVE MY OWN CONFESSION of having a bit of narcissism in me, we all do! Being a little narcissistic has become a part of society. This term is not to be taken lightly and if you think you may be then there is a chance you are not. But we are creating a society that feels that way because the human feeling has been taken out of the equation, as I perceive it to be that we have become numb and angry. When I look at those times when I have wanted people to change, or to push life to go my way, I am stepping into a place of "all about me." Did I think of the consequences of getting my own way as manipulating others? Changing another's view by telling the story how I want to tell it, for the unconscious desire to either be the victim or to sit in my place of self-pity. Life is not all about me!

We have come to use narcissistic language too freely at times. We make a choice to label someone as narcissistic because we keep pushing ourselves into their lives, even when they have time and time again told us that they want something different or have a different view. We sometimes push others to accept our power even if they have said "No," because we have our mind made up that this person "has" to be in our life. Who else has done this? I know I have! Then, when I would see these people in healthy relationships I would think, something has to be wrong. I look back at this version of myself and can now see that the story I was telling for many years was from my "poor me" syndrome or my "I want," mindset! Why would I ever want to face my role and my pushy ways? What if I had listened to all the messages, they had been providing me with since the beginning, walked away, and made a choice to thank them for their honesty? Maybe I would not have met life with such resistance and could have had a healthy story from the start. Damn it, I would not have a book to write then and so many stories to rewrite.

I never want to be the Guide that portrays the whole image that being spiritual means, "You are perfect" or that "You have done nothing wrong" in your life. That every day is full of sunshine and blooming flowers, as this is a false reality and it is okay to have a shitty day! God forbid I could even be that delusional! You see, I base my work around portraying myself as real, vulnerable, and always willing to tell the story of my life experiences, even though some are not that pretty. I have found myself in the past few months faced with situations and attacks on who I am, and how I am showing up in this world. I have found myself going through some real emotional struggles with the shifting direction in my career, changes in my health, and some past emotions that keep rising up in my life. I even let the judgement of my writing stand in the way, so I stopped writing for a period of time. Imagine if that person only knew how hard writing is when you live with a neurological disease that is affecting all your fine motor skills. This all has been magnified by the fact that I continue to work on myself by asking other professionals to assist me through my human experiences.

The one thing that keeps coming to light through all of this for me, is how to be "okay," as I feel and work my way through all of these emotions, putting them into perspective. I feel so loved, from a place so deep within me, that it took years to find, and is protected by something so much bigger than myself. This is my truth, that I love!

Knowing that my fear is ego, I still find myself occasionally back in that place of, "What if I am not good enough?" I had let someone else's judgement get in, and for a moment it had affected me. But not today! Today I step forward and try again! For you see, even though I am a medium I am human! Even though I am a mother I am human! We are all human and trying our best to show up, and as long as we continue to believe we are good enough and just show up, we are doing something that is of service to our spirit. My spiritual life comes from living true to me, to my continually changing beliefs, to be honest with myself and speak my truth. Let no one question your connection to your God consciousness, let no one take your power, and continue to do as much good in the time you live upon this earth as you possibly can!

I had been a survivalist, which has been my get by, but does not work in the world of existing. Nothing today is as I saw it yesterday, for it is as if God has lifted me up out of it. Like a helicopter coming in to rescue us. I guess in a way, I was saved! Omg! In this very "ah ha" moment, I just realized I got "saved." At the end of my day I bathed, then just prior to crawling into bed heard, "Take a sleeping pill," as a poor sleeper this would fully take me out and help me sleep. In the morning, I woke to the realization that everything is different. I thought, "Maybe my messages of being saved had been true?" They were true to where I was, but now all has changed. The filters of reality after you meet the Savior is different, I am in a new reality.

Today this is my reality, and a truth that has been hard to face. From here, until the end, I will remain in the glow of my golden light, still standing at the gates, but my desire to leave this earth sooner does not exist in the truth I live today. I faced the truth of my human posttraumatic stress disorder (PTSD) and self-absorbed reality with love, so I could then be the real me in my work, my life, and in this book from beginning to end. This section was written at the end of an era on January 31st, 2019, as this day was the true end. Many years from the beginning of the stories told at three years old, for now I am real and realize the reality of my truth. The truth of my reality is this is usually about the time I quit and walk away from my fear of success and fear of love. The things that most people draw towards, I had been running away from, to return to the land of mediocre. The place I could shine but never grow. The *More Than Existing self-actualization* program and the commitment to never back down has pulled me past the threshold of no return, and past the fear of unconsciousness.

While in a place of love today, I found myself returning to the comfort of what appears as if, or actually is, a selfish little narcissistic moment, of the narcissist in me that starts with the action of real human anxiety, and not a hit to answer the call of the spirit world. Those calls are the easiest to answer, but this was a call for awareness that rose from the core of my human existence. That call led me to the image of the crazy, cold bitch, who has a seat in the swamp of my tears and in the darkness behind the heart, unaware of my reality that I believed to be healed. She returned the moment my daughter and granddaughter needed me the most, as I looked at the ultrasound screen and saw my beautiful grandbaby. My heart flooded with joy, but my tears turned to ice, as I felt myself return to the day I could see in my meditation, but had created a story to hide my truth of avoiding the discomfort and running, as I had to leave her and go to the place that the skin may never crack. As I found myself losing my breath, my new truth was unfolding and a vision from the past came flooding back. The girl who is never there through your pain, to stand up and speak out for others, has always had a little of the survival instinct to just run and barely exist. I went to my place of comfort, inward to a place of familiarity and safety, and left the reality that we would have to face together, to the one soul who should have always been able to count on me.

I had seen the fight and flight behavior way too many times through the eyes of my mother, and through her mother. The story I told, as she was yelling at me, when I was fading away from alcohol poisoning in the back of a paddy wagon at thirteen, was not about the face or angry words of a self-centered woman, it was the words and energy of fear from a voice that had experienced more than her share of pain, anger, and sadness. The reality of her truth was nothing of the story I heard and witnessed. She has been by my side guiding me, and the narcissist in me, the victim and the villain, would now have to end the show. This is the end but a beginning of seeing what the narcissist in me has done, for in my meditation this too I now shall see.

I have tremendous love for my daughter and my future granddaughter and would give them my last breath. But in this moment, I was not giving my daughter what she needed the most during her ultrasound. What she needed was my attention and the sense of security a mother bear brings in the moments when trauma is about to reappear.

At the age of three I abandoned myself. When my daughter was three, I emotionally abandoned a piece of her, out of my fear of losing her, all as a punishment to myself, and a sense of lack of worth, for my actions took away what she had wanted the most, a brother. Now, back at the ultrasound and looking into the eyes of her soon to be born baby girl, and seeing the essence of my son, I made a promise. Today, I promise you that, "Through your challenges, pains, and great successes, I will not just be there for you, but for your momma." Today I end another cycle. Today it just gets real, and from here on I have to move and shift gears, because the reality is that life is not all butterflies and rainbows, but there is always magic in the signs of all that appear to remind us. We left the hospital, speaking of her brother I had been blessed to see, in the image of the ultrasound. Together we walked on a pedway of glass, exposed, and vulnerable, looking at a faded painted rainbow with all its colors visible but well worn, walking over the bridge of metaphors, symbols, and signs from a world I know so well. The comfort of a heaven I knew I had often begged for, to escape this human reality, to leave my pain, and pour over onto the one who I had already given more than enough of my life of heartache and pain. The realization of all I had seen in my mother, I was seeing in me, as she had seen in hers. But as gifted healers, we had a little too much ego to believe that the pain was someone else's and not ours to carry and spew, and instead did as we were conditioned to do continuing to carry the burdens.

But not today! Today, I have a truth to tell and it is not one of pain, it is of one who finally understands peace and love. For I had always been gifted someone who could never be replaced, and now the selfless act I shall do today is set the spirit of a grandmother free, as I heard her yell loud enough to wake me up, "Set my girls free!" With the ultimate act of kindness, love, and compassion I finally set her free. In visiting my grandmother during what I was not to humanly know at the time was our last visit, she could see I was pregnant with my daughter. I could see her light fading and had said to my mother that I knew in my heart I would never see her in human form again. But the burden I carried was my then selfish heart had not enough sense to sit and tell her that my love for her was eternal. In that moment, just as she did to me tonight, I heard, "She will be Maggie." I could not understand then, but today I know all too well, and the words of judgement was not that of her real truth, as I will now walk beside my daughter and the circle of love and strength of powerful women that has now returned. She placed me just long enough in the sadness and pain until I could understand and have compassion, until I could pinpoint my eternal sadness in a life, I had everything to live for.

My narcissist shadow inside, who wanted to own and be responsible for everything, including what my granddaughter was experiencing, was now understanding her cries for help were unheard because my strongest gift of strength, was also my weakness. Due to my inability or unwillingness to trust, I made a choice that cost me everything, and the price that was paid, was paid by more than myself. Today I speak a truth and I surrender it all over. I graciously accept my gift of gold. My awareness to the name of my pain I guess would be PTSD and my avoidance of life was not that I was a party pooper, it was in all a real truth that I could not take a single moment more of feeling cold and numb. Today I will be the strength with some weakness, but I will stand in the circle, as a healer, a mother, and a woman, and today the circle will be unbroken. Today are you ready to get real?

CHAPTER 10

The gates of the glow and the glory

AT THE GATE AND GLOW I realized there was no celebration of sparkling lights, but a satisfaction that touched my soul. The truth and light within, has been an illusion of all of what I thought my life would be, or what I thought I was here to create. As I woke with the sense of release within my whole self, I feel I have woken to an unfamiliar but safe place, a place where the building blocks and stable parts of the foundation I have been building were an illusion of the existence I had been living. They are the safety net of the world I had created to be accepted, to be a part of a world where we have created a let's come together, but let's be separate, divided sense of who we are, and why we are forever on the search for something beyond ourselves. Something that makes us feel anything, whether it is completeness, emptiness, fullness, whatever it may be, for when we feel nothing, we feel lost. What if the rawness of feeling nothing, is the place of where you learn everything? What if the sense of having nothing fulfilling those human needs, is exactly the place we need to be? To get to be uncomfortable, and learn to be comfortable, because in this place you have no expectations of an outcome to a life you have been taught to create. To map out, manifest a future, create goals, have dreams, and maybe find the road that leads you to your destination or disappointment, however you may want to look at it. What if you and your empty self are experiencing exactly what no one has yet to understand? That getting to the point of "nothing" is the key to happiness, the road to eternal happiness that we look to the outside to discover, when truly it was to be fully discovered on the inside. For the blank canvas is the creation of the greatness, of a world of no expectations, and a fulfillment of something greater. For this is the universal feeling, where time and space does not matter, for the world beyond the existence and the ever-expanding expansion of space without reality, is the freeing sense of opening. The clearing of the junk within our own space is the beginning of enlightenment. Of not needing to replace what is not missing, knowing that the vast universe has already provided all that it needs, to complete and fulfill the journey that awaits.

Take a moment, close your eyes, and imagine a clear universe, a floating sense of you. In this space try moving around. Is it easier than you thought? Why? Perhaps the effortless float determined the destination of the freedom awaiting you. Freedom is an awareness that opening the doors and gates belong to you, and not others. Therefore, to float effortlessly, you cannot be tied to people and stories. Sound a little selfish, with a tinge of narcissistic tendency? If that thought popped in your head, then no! When we become done, it is not abandonment of those we love, its learning we are as valuable, as those we love. The golden glow becomes apparent when we love ourselves as much as we love others. You do not have to own anyone's bullshit! You are not selfish, you are selfless and sometimes faceless. As you navigate and weave your way through a world that can feel broken and damaged, you somehow have placed yourself in front of those who have been broken and damaged and are not of good intentions.

I sat in a belief that those who harmed me with their actions and words, I owed everything that I was finding to fill my soul.

Like repaying a debt, I would apologize for what I did not do and accept that they were justified in their selfish attack, because of their bad day or made up stories, as I was reflecting a person from their past. I had taken the many incredible pieces of me and left it all with people who today at this point, do not deserve to hold, for they held me accountable for what they could not fix on their own. You have created an image around being selfless, a martyr to the cause, living disconnected and alone from your own needs and desires. The need to be needed and claiming the fame of being selfless, may be your so-called misunderstood passion, but the trauma response of the pleaser will at some point be your poison. The ego has us irresistible and irritating all at the same time, and this is not golden in the light of our worth, so as a result our glow begins to tarnish. The key to the gate is love, and just as we desire a quiet space in a busy home, so does your soul desire space to sit with you.

The story is now old and was never the truth, it was the anxious desire of what appeared to be an act of love. It is the facade of the past, of old wounds and healing, the reality of an unhealthy, selfish desire to fulfill the insecurities and fears, using the eyes of another. The third person disassociation of my truth had now been met with my light, so where do we go from here? The darkness of the old has lifted, and the rays of the now have opened an opportunity to rejoin the missing part of your soul. That which you had no idea was missing, but that you thought was just the sense that you were not from this world, in truth you were just incomplete, but now with your soul in place, you are complete. You are no longer the gem that those who do not deserve get to hold onto because you make them feel safe, or you satisfy a moment in their life of misery, leaving you with the attachment of what they can no longer carry. You are here now to be reconnected with that other part of your soul, with the one that opens the space to let your guard down, to be selfless instead of selfish. This is your time to be unstuck from an old belief and be open to a love that is felt without touch, known without words, given without asking, and protected without protection. You are now free to love without words and be loved without expectation.

"Welcome, the wise woman of wisdom," was the message I would receive. For in the light of loving my shadows, I had discovered a truth in my soul that the pieces of me I was giving away was the pieces I actually loved the most. In the darkness of my shadows, and then topped by the insecurities and fear of others, I had lost the connection and direction that had always appeared in my dreams. That powerhouse I saw with a beautiful smile and a glow in her eyes was me. I expected that other people's desire to need me, would someday be enough to pull me to the light. I had to travel to the root cause of this, where I was awakened to the voice of the Lilith in me, as I dropped to the underworld way beyond the glow of light, but well secured to the golden thread of hope and faith. I reached the twinning part of me that I had long pushed away as evil, bad, or too much for my little town to accept. I hid my relationship to God, to the medium in me, and the gifted that to this day are still under the attacks of the fearful. Those on a witch hunt to shush us from awakening the hearts and desires of all to live a life in the light. I had placed a lot of expectations upon myself, but very little upon others accompanying me, wishing to walk by my side. The expectation now, was to reach out and up to grab on to the line of rescue and leave no part of me behind. For how would I ever heal if I did not take all of my shadow with me, to walk slightly behind and to always be walking through the trail of my light and through my love. As I guide others to heal, I will only look back to remind my shadow that she is loved, and that the glow is always hers, but the leader through the gate that all the world will see, will be the truest essence of me, bathed in the light.

To allow this woman to come to life would end up being the most selfless act of kindness and compassion that I would ever do. It can be the kindest thing you will do for you! Why? Because you are going to be given an opportunity to tap into your own wise woman, or at this point I have come to accept that my work is for all to tap into the wisdom within themselves. Welcoming my wise woman had never been about the money, the glory, desire to be right, or to bring others down, it was about releasing the "I am sorry," for ever thinking I should hide any part of me, especially the parts that truly needed to fit in the light, feel the warmth of the love and see its reflection in the glow of the God consciousness inside of me. It has been about the desire to be heard, to be respected while being respectful and compassionate, and without losing the compassion for myself. The journey has been about asking the right questions and experiencing a courageous life by taking responsibility and walking through the flames of desire and passion for a life I know is the life of the wise man, woman, and child inside of us all.

We are the beacons of light in a world that has been dulled and not just by others, but by us! From our conditioned fears and insecurities, we forgot something! We forgot us! We forgot that the Goddesses did not follow behind hidden but have always walked beside. Not dressed for battle but dressed for success. The battle is over and now the reality of life has begun. As I teach from a place of leading like Jesus, I remember the pivotal meeting so many years ago, where I was taken to place the crown on his head. I knew from this point on that the struggles would still appear until the end of my time. But I honor the promise I made to trust, as he would remind me that a leader is always following, and a follower is always a leader to another. As you remember your truth, what would you truly like to lead your people to? A gate that traps or a gate that will open and allow the love to flow?

Someone will have to always have the courage to walk slightly ahead, and as I was handed a staff out of a gift of gratitude, I knew I was being prepared to walk the journey of the archetype of Moses, setting the people I had held accountable and responsible for my life free, as I forgave and allowed the light within to direct not dictate. You are the essence of all things worthy of the light, and as you can see in the beginning and until the end, the human in me has had to endure. She will continue to be thrown to the world of the fated, but my faith and knowing that sitting closest to the gates of opportunities, instead of back in the darkness of the past, will provide the best chance of catching the golden key when you are reaching out.

The reward of it all is the success of being seen and heard. The success to stop the judgement, ridicule, and blame, and own that shit! The reward of seeing true beauty, dignity, and the right to your own identity. The success to show up and shine in whatever and whomever you choose to be. The success of health and abundance of a well-rounded, wealthy life.

CHAPTER 11

The weight of our words

AS I SIT TO WRITE this chapter, I find myself spiraling a little to the back of my heart towards my spine, representing the tree of life.

Feeling an intense rage rising as I am consciously aware of my desire to write this book from a place of love and understanding, but as it's told from where I am in life, I am also very honest with myself about where I have been and that my human self is still triggered by some things. I am not perfect but am truly realistic! This realness is my vulnerability, baring a scarred heart and face that is hard to hide. Words that flow through the tunnels of my ears and scan past my human eyes still trigger the irrational, but also rational self. In this moment of writing, the rage triggered inside my soul has been brought about through the actions of keyboard warriors within the cyber world, who have placed judgmental stories upon some kick ass women. The human truths of personal opinions have come flying out, amplified by the angry and foggy view of eyes that still have a closed view of acceptance.

The words we utter are an internal reflection of ourselves. I pause here to utter a word of love and a shoutout to the talents of Jay-lo, Shakira and Demi Laveto, as they gave their all in their performance and still passed on a message without rage. Their message was one of peace, love, happiness, and owning that there is nothing wrong with being a strong, sexy Goddess! I for one would kill to have a body like that and their talent! These women empowered and supported each other, instead of trashing. Everyone is entitled to their opinions, but opinions can be like assholes and you may know the truth to that one. In that moment of pounding the keyboard or opening our mouths, what are we really wanting to say? When we are in a moment of this social ganging up and picking sides, step back and look at what is really unfolding. Maybe go back and watch again and again, until you can find one good thing, one kind word, one moment of praise, that may change it all for you. Ask, "What do I really feel about my own reaction? Who are my words truly reflecting?"

I remember apologizing for my so called "inappropriate" clothing that would show a little too much skin, or a shirt that showed I have cleavage. The words I utter a lot today is, "Get over yourself!" That message is sometimes for me, as I look in the mirror and the judgement of my mother's fears race back to my head. Words hurt, and I have a lifetime of words that trigger like a loaded slingshot, but unable to take down a giant as they had been words dampening the spirit of a child, a young teenager, a single mother and all else. The anger that had festered inside my head and heart became the words I would try to justify, apologize for, and sometimes lash out, but always quick to take back when becoming aware.

The words I would stuff down to the bottom, instead of standing up and spilling the words back out, would be added to the weight of my food. Carefully chosen to experience the crunch of the anger, and sooth my soul with its warmth and comfort. Until the mirror reflection looking back, started to speak as my mother spoke to me. The words I uttered to myself became as angry as hers, as I was becoming the reflection. I ate back the words with vengeance and spewed them out with a jab down my throat, violently throwing up the pain of unsaid words. Then came the moment of satisfaction mixed with disgust, as I looked in the mirror and the words came rushing back. I would wipe my face and step out into the battlefield of words uttered from a world of hurt children dressed up as adults. Adults who battled the world in an attempt to be seen and heard, all while hiding behind the protection of the false truth of reality.

As I think of the words uttered today, the anger of judgement towards women rise up again. How fucking dare we judge women, or anyone who works so hard to be amazing! How dare we judge a woman brave enough to get up and get dressed today! How dare we judge anyone who bravely stands in their power for anyone still too afraid to shine! Words hurt when they come from the mouths of the vindictive and hurt more when coming from the mouths of those pretending to be okay. Words help heal the world when they come from the mouth of those with good intentions in their heart.

My words back to a society of shaming, blaming and judgement is now, "Fuck you!" Yes, my words matter as does the voice that comes out and yes, angry projection gets us nowhere, but there will be times when you must stand up and have those ugly human moments. It will not be pretty, and as a last attempt to suppress you, you may hear back the gaslighting judgement accepting it for the last time. Take it from me, you may do the same as I had to do. When that happens, take a deep breath, turn on those heals and with your now straight spine walk away, as you do, trust me you may chuckle, and you will smile, because for once your words mattered and from that point on you may start to realize, you matter.

When you realize you matter, that all people matter, you will choose your words more carefully. You will choose when, and how, they need to count to make a stand. With love for yourself and for the love you feel in you. Martin Luther King as angry as he must of been under a suppression that I can only imagine from the stories of my first nation family, feel sure that when he was in the safety of those who cared deeply, that he may have let it all spew out. He knew words mattered when uttered out into the world, spoken with great love. To this day you can still hear the echo of that love in his words, "Today, I have a dream."

Today I have a dream! When I started to write this book, before it ever had a word on paper, my internal anger and self-sabotage became the heart that remembered these very words, and my anger came out as, "I am done!" Then and only then, could it become a desire to discover a love inside of myself to heal and grow towards the dream life that projected and changed my words of hate and anger to a desire to inspire with love.

I was done stuffing shit down, jabbing the inside of my throat, rewarding my secret win with a throw up of unchewed food, only to look back in a mirror where nothing in the reflection had changed but the words had cut deeper. This moment did not appear until I saw the reflection today of the anger I had of a woman I believed to be a mentor and a goddess, judge the powerhouses who took the stage at Super Bowl 2020. In that moment I was not angry at her, but at myself, for through her eyes I saw a healer and up until a few months prior to the completion of this book, I had still secretly jabbed my throat every time I would speak a truth or take a stand for myself, after which I would be judged. My love within kept it from being a regular habit for too long, but a human moment of uttered words was always enough to forget I mattered.

"Choose your words wisely," they say. "Speak from a place that hurts no one," they say. "Speak your truth," they say. What no one says, is that you will have to deal with the consequences of how those you are trying to communicate with receive the messages. Texting is not a form of reliable communication, but a coward's way of speaking a lot of anger and fear that attaches itself to an energy which serves no one. A heart cannot speak a truth through a digital cyber world. A heart can only be felt through the touch of the hand, a joining of the body, and a look into the eyes. Go back and look into the eyes of those your words hurt, including yourself. Today, start changing the words and make sorry, forgiveness, and love some of those words. Life's about vulnerability, openness, and unconditional acceptance that moments will happen, and they may not be pretty or smart, but they are all a part of the human, shadow self, and the joining and building of any relationship. We all arrived into the world a little broken within our human form, but we all come into a relationship in a whole, well put together spirit. Knowing full well how to love, and how to care when our spirits are meant to join. The problem with the human is we become afraid. The fears of our past relationships and life experiences creep into the healing wounds and expose the darkness that had been healing, but still not enough to have complete faith and trust.

What I have learned in the experience of my now broken, but healed heart, is to never assume a story of fear that escalates into a mountain you cannot climb. Never build or break a relationship on the false bravery of a text message. Use your true voice, so your real truth comes out and not the fear that you have not yet healed. Never be too big to apologize for your role in a situation that has gone bad, even when the heart is hurt, and the ego is bruised. Be patient and kind, and never let a moment to know love slip away because of a bruised ego, or because of the quick snap of anger that can so bravely fall into a place of misspoken words and failed communication.

The failed communication started with the conversations I had with myself, the stories I would tell, and the words I would then believe. The day I started to pay attention to my words, and the words I was reflecting unto others, was the day I sat and started a conversation of how I was going to do more for me, be kinder with myself, and stand up to the biggest bully in my life, ME! A martyr to the cause of self-righteousness, I started to see, as I had seen it reflected back at me behind my back with words that would seep through the cracks, aimed through the mouths of the hurting, were words that were never the same as they came from the mouth, at the place of origin. Amazing how the anger will pray on the hurting to inflict more hurt, while still trying to convince the world and themselves that they are the savior and healer, who will always be there to jump in and save the world in its time of need. Still sticking daggers in the hearts of those who did not need them, but still loved them just because they saw the light inside.

As you can see reflected in this whole chapter, my real and vulnerable self is at the point in the writings where I was still very much on a journey, and I still am, even after the end of a belief, that we have a long way to go before our ego self can move past our instant ability to speak or write before we think. Oh, the things that cannot be taken back!

This is the point where the break water broke and the flow began to change, placed here in chapter 11 unintentionally by myself but intentionally well planned by my channel and protectors. As I believe at this point of putting it all together and reading my own words, that I have achieved a new level of awareness. As you read, you will discover many points that may trigger the same in you, and that is okay! You are okay, and there will be days when it is okay to not be okay.

"I am sorry for allowing my fear of hurt and deceit of the past to be so in control, that I could not separate myself from the ego and pain long enough to see past the story created, and have the patience to wait for the communication of a real conversation. I love you with all of me, miss you like crazy, and am sorry you got the worst of me during the times I had been scraping up the many pieces of the best of me." This was a note I thought I had written for my now partner, but as I read it back, I realized I wrote this to myself.

I had written him many stories, notes, and letters of anger, that I now realize were notes to myself. I had been one of the angry people, and I was reflecting my pain out at him. I would be honestly believing that my keyboard warrior had every right to spew over onto him all that he was doing "wrong" to me. This was one of the gentler messages where I realized in reading, that my pain and hurt were so deep that I was healing through using him as my reflection because facing myself would be the hardest to do. The humbling and the freedom that comes when we stop lashing out at those who try to love us, be it our partners, friends, children, or the world in general, will set us free.

I am not the cause of your hurt, but I may be the reflection of the hurt inside of you, and as a healer I had become that for so many. This is how the hurt actions of so many became the hurt I would carry in my hands and in my heart. As you read this, I will not put myself up on a pedestal of righteousness and say, "I would never have done that!" Fuck, we all have! As you take a good look at your life and the words you have written, spoken, and thought, my hope is that from this point on you can start to recognize how we reject our own fears and lack of self-worth on to others.

I had been the reflection of the rich kid who bullied one of my ex's, and he made sure I was going to pay the emotional price for the bad behavior of another, and in some sick way we are all doing this. Becoming aware starts the change, accountability changes the majority, and the acceptance that you are human, leaves room to apologize when we have moments that trigger us. The awareness of your words opens up the truth about the importance of communication, and the value of healing the past so that another human is not the third person reflection of all that is wrong in your healing journey, but a valuable asset to the joy in your life.

I was a reflection for my mother for so many issues within her life and from where we sit now, some I can shake my head and laugh at, but to my inner child it took me to the depth of my pain and self-inflicted suffering. I was a sponge for the words and not a deflection of the reflection. My eating disorder started at the age of three in all honesty and not at the, "If you just lose ten pounds," story. I had a picture in my head of how fat I must have been, and anger for what we all blocked, behind a truth we could not see as words reflected by the story. Just another third person survival skill of reflection that we all do. The words were my mother's, the reflection my mother's, and I was her third person story. I was safe and never leaving her no matter how much the words hurt.

I was taken by my mother to "Slimdown" and sat in the unbroken circle of not good enough women striving in desperation to improve their lives with a diet and not a mental repair. They were all reflections of another story I did not know, but each and every one was a grown woman with a reflection of my mother in the years to come. A love/hate relationship that would be our reflection for years. The day we talked about me writing this part, she said she didn't take me to Slimdown because she thought I was fat, she took me because she thought she was fat and did not want to go alone. My mother laughed uncontrollably as I told her of her destruction through telling my story as I saw it, and then I laughed with her. That young mom is gone, and a truth that unfolded of our lack of connection as mother and daughter (we were more like sisters) has become clearer than ever now that communication is taking place, and the words I can now use with her are loving, instead of wanting to get back at her for what she did not do for me.

As I look back at my life and compare this to so many stories I have heard and helped heal, I feel mine were so minor, but they were not. They were life changing for me, as I spent the early years of my life being raised by a young mom who was fearful and brave all at the same time and a dad who was living in a, "Man's world of freedom of the era." My mom had been abused, raised in poverty, raped, and had undiagnosed ADHD. My childhood consisted of me being the second child, born ten months after my sibling who never slept, so definitely not the child she had time for. My life, my story, became conditioned to believe that someone else's needs were more important than my own. I took being emotionally abused with harsh words and being called stupid, and a goodyear blimp as acceptable.

In my view, my mother had an issue with "fat" being disgusting, and of course I was not the petite tiny girl, so she would remind me of how much prettier I would look, "Ten pounds lighter." I entered my first Slimdown meeting and spelt out the word, sat in the circles, and shame talked about our issues of weight. That was the beginning of what would become years of extreme exercise, dieting, anorexia, and bulimia. My work now I hope is to show and share love and compassion to women who don't need any more harsh words and judgement, but have instead been inspired to change themselves by going back to the root of the problem, where we find our light, repair the foundation, and see the light in those who tried their best. If we want to change ourselves, then those before us cannot be the doormats to our victimhood and we cannot continue to let others wipe their dirt off on us. I am still under the microscope of visual appearance by my mother and others, but now its ok because I am okay, and I am aware of my emotional relationship with food.

The desire to be healthy physically, reflects for me a desire to be healthy emotionally. The words I followed back with food and weighted down, I now remove with movement. The fire in me is a desire to move forward, and I am not to be a door mat or a bookend, but the key to the door and the bestselling book on the shelf. My words of love I promise myself, will echo love and light throughout the world, for now they shall have value. Becoming light as a feather to fly but landing with enough weight to help the heart of another.

I know the weight of the struggle and I have been at the end of it all, struggling through my skinniest as I did my heaviest, and the anger still found its way in. During the thinnest years, the pain was easier to hide because I looked great, now I have words of faith, hope, and encouragement. I have a desire and thanks to a good friend, "The Word Alchemist," I have a whole new relationship with words. When you have faith in yourself, your faith aligns to the thoughts in your head, because your words will be your truth and not others. You will appreciate the impact and trigger others with love and acceptance, instead of pushing away opportunities. Today say a kind word to your reflection, a kind word to another, and most of all do not reflect your anger and judgement on anyone. Take a good look at those words before you hit send! But if you need to say "fuck" today in your sentence, make it count!

CHAPTER 12

To you I am sorry

"THE ROSE," SANG BY LEANNE Rimes was playing, and my heart felt love for the ones who loved me along the journey to the best of their abilities. The ones who tried, and I refused to let in from a place of fear, protection, and lack of worth. To the teachers and unknown messengers of love who would randomly walk up and say the right thing at the right time, I am so thankful, but sorry that I could not at the time see what you could see. I am sorry it had taken me until the end of this book to see my worth. The rose is the Mother Mary of transformation and unconditional love, who has stayed by my side throughout this journey of transformation, and as I listen to a voice of an angel and the choir behind her, I know that the skies of heaven and the light of God is blessing me today and every day. That billboard with my name in lights, has been my freewill choice to plug in and light up, just as it is yours.

I had started a journey with Mother Mary so long ago while on a trip to Sedona. That trip was to be what I once again thought would bring me enlightenment and a vision of clear direction. It brought me through trails and mountains, through the hot desert with a person who was not interested in the spiritual journey but the photography, and who I felt had been most impatient then, but patient now in this time. I believe there was a real truth unfolding of an end we were not ready to let go of, because of the uncomfortable truth that this was better than being alone. We drove there for me, as it was to be my experience, and as I reflect back to it now, there were so many moments for me that had become the signs from heaven in a place I know I have lived and died many times.

This trip was no different, as I walked through the desert into a vortex of masculine energy towards a landmark that looked nothing as I thought it would. Circling the rocks in the heat, I came upon a place to sit peacefully in the stillness, where I felt I could not be seen, and I could not see those frustrated by the heat, until the moment came when he spotted me, and the fury of words and panic came flying out. I felt it as a hit to my heart, but also as an awareness that the words were spoken in fear and not as it appeared in anger, as he did care about my safety. There would always be that feeling to some degree, I think. That moment of getting out of the desert and back to the car felt as if I knew that the only way back to my peace, was to pray to God to show me the way. The "sorry" for holding an anger in my heart for that experience, and many other moments, was not coming that day or any time soon, and that was my truth. I had a shutdown gauge, and am usually patient, but that day I was only sorry I had this person walking on my spiritual journey with me. I am kind and forgiving, but I am not a saint! I was sorry I had nothing left inside of me to help him, because what he needed at the time, I needed more.

The moments continued, and as I stopped to talk with a sweet old Russian lady, asking for things to do in the area to please what I felt was an agitated man, I was asked by her, "Why are you here? What about what you want?" Her response took me back, as I smiled. The irritation continued and the unfolding of angry circumstances carried on, as I found myself sitting on a hill across from a church I wanted to enter so badly to feel the Holy's.

As I sat and looked at the magnitude of beauty in the rocks, I heard a voice telling me to, "Come, look under the trees." I started looking around the bases of the broken tree trunks and within moments I was a kid again, feeling joy and happiness. The next moments to unfold, changed it all, and was the moment of the true beginnings of another book in the making titled "You Can't Make This Shit Up." I had spotted a white rock on top of what looked like the grave of an animal, covered by some fallen trees. Being curious I had to touch it, but as I reached a hand out, I heard the voice again, "Corrie don't touch. Walk around and look into my eyes." I listened, and went around, only to discover it was the statue of Mother Mary. In that moment I dropped to the ground and a flood of tears fell. A string of synchronicities had taken me to this place that she had been guiding me to, and I was obviously listening. She told me to have faith and that she would guide me on the journey I was about to take. "Do not take me from here," I heard Mother Mary speak, "for I am not yours to take. Place this moment in your heart, and trust all that will show you your way." I felt sorry in that moment for wanting to take that which was placed to light up another and wanting to claim it all for myself to light up my soul. We have all been at this place, where we have wanted to take what is not ours, in order to fill a hole within. With a love I could not explain, I took that moment and placed it in my heart, knowing that more moments would still need to come before I would finally break free to the peace within, and the freedom of surrender.

The messengers of the trip would appear, in the faces of those I would not expect, yet all of this was still not enough for me to stop the pain and struggles I continued to inflict upon myself, but the journey was well on its way. Apologies did not need to be said to Mother Mary, or any of the guides and angels who I thought would have to be getting frustrated by now! The apology was meant for me, as I was sorry that I could not see what they had all seen! I was in such a hurry to get there, to get anywhere, and to share all that I had learned, but I still needed to learn the biggest lesson, my own worth and value. Am I ever sorry that I let it all be so unimportant, and most of all in letting myself be the least important. I have now stopped to smell the roses and look around in awe of the life I am blessed to live. Now I say, "Thank you," instead of, "I am sorry," for I have found the strength to forgive, but not forget.

We are the light, and only die when we cut ourselves off from the root of the growth, and shadow ourselves by moving away from the source of the light within and above us all.

Today I write the "I am sorry," that came long before the forgiveness. The forgiveness came like a slow release, all the way through the journey as my story was told, up until the day this book was close to completion. Forgiveness came in a dream where I could finally let go of my unborn son. Through my writing I learned to fully forgive myself for allowing my pain to be projected unto the woman who cared for my needs, and to myself I am sorry that what I wrote eleven years ago, took me until now to fully believe and understand.

Today as if I am plugging in a billboard sign displaying my name in lights, I now see I have both greatness and weakness, and hold myself and others close, just as Mother Mary held close her son as she supported with love the journey Jesus was destined to take, and that which she could not change. Today, we have a freewill choice of our own struggle, but not the fated human pain that will have to be experienced by us all, so why carry and cause ourselves extra pain that we are conditioned to believe is ours to carry?

Before recognizing that I was worthy of any level of forgiveness, I had to find words of acceptance. Learning to embrace "I am sorry," was the acceptance of my own journey of building and destroying any and all worth in life. I started to question the good and the bad in so many things, asking "Why me?" The answer was not as I wanted to hear, but it came through as simple as, "Why not?" As humans, we were never to be left out of the beauty and the pain, as all would show up regardless, and cleaning will always have to take place. It took me years to discover Ho'oponopono and what "cleaning" really meant, which was not packing up the past and placing the clutter in boxes to be stored out of site, but still in your life. It was about the true principals of cleaning and declaring, "I see you. I forgive you. I hear you." Words of validation that we are all worthy enough to let go of our garbage instead of passing it on to someone else.

Try giving away something you love instead of something you are tired of. Not that easy is it? So why do we hang on, drag around, and continue to lay blame? Cleaning means clearing and clearing takes work. Saying, "I am sorry" is a cleaner not an eraser that clears it away. It is the start of a process that starts in the level easiest to reach and ends in the level hardest to get to. "Sorry I did not see your worth," is a validation I know I will acknowledge. This has taken me eleven years, many declarations of "I am sorry," and excuses before I could reach the forgiveness I had found in the glimpses buried deep within the clutter of my old stories.

Cleaning is an outlet for my words, behaviors, and actions that remain unspoken, still being processed, created as distractions from the pain, or that I was conditioned to believe. For that I am sorry it has been passed on, but not sorry to teach the importance of cleaning up your shit! Sorry means nothing without action and the action is yours to take. I look back to where *More Than Existing* started and am sorry that I was not willing to give my all to the forgiveness chapter. That piece would need to wait until the end of the story, and then be reflected back to the beginning. There has been and always will be, a time to go back to the basics to view, review, clean and declutter. Damn, I even moved houses and relocated to a new city this time, but still managed to drag the things I was not ready to part with. For that I apologize to my higher self for not listening at the time.

This is the stage when returning to the basement is crucial in order to find the cracks in your foundation. The empire you wish to build, I can guarantee will crumble if it is still weak, and I am sorry you are still filling in the cracks. Sorry is a powerful word, and saying it as unapologetic for just being you and being present, or from the unawareness of the habit that has taken away its value, will cause the real "I am sorry," to bare no weight, no value, and the repeated word will slip right on by never hitting your own heart. Betrayal at the ultimate level is forgiving everyone else but not yourself, the next betrayal is saying "I am sorry," if you do not mean it. Make your apologies count!

CHAPTER 13

The contracts we sign

I HAVE TAKEN A STEP back to review my own relationships and understanding of soul and human contracts. I found myself hearing the chatter in my head during the stages of being a child, a teenager, and a pleaser to the comfort of others, and a discomfort to me. As with all souls, the challenges will be real, and we have all met our fair share. My desire to communicate from the consciously awaken woman and not the anxious, erotic, temper flaring, frustrated old self, would not be easy as memories are habits taking physical action, like a rebel against a cause.

I am here to learn trust, but also to find a voice from the lost languages and oppression of those that walked before us, contracted to bring life and animation to the voice I have been given in this lifetime.

As you may remember from reading in a previous chapter, we are usually much braver with typing and hitting send, then having vocal conversations. Yes, I have come to realize my reflection was in that of those keyboard warriors with the fingers of shame and blame. I did this to my parents as hiding behind them was my safe place. Oh yes, they were in this contract to raise me, to have the patience to raise a mixture of this introvert, extrovert, empath, and all-knowing old soul, who would have to learn she knew nothing about being a human. She was contracted to learn to listen beyond the human and from that place she has learned love, but just because she could read minds did not mean she knew the truth.

When you stop and look at all who have been placed in your life, there are many experiences, and yes some we definitely could have done without as they were horrible to go through. It is our freewill choice, to choose whether we grow, heal, or stay in the story. We will always have to live with the story, but not of it, yes, a contract can be completed as you undo the responsibility of the ownership for the behaviors and habits of others. It is your freewill choice whether you take ownership and responsibility for your desire to stay mushroomed because of the experience or choose to rise to the top and look in with new eyes.

The stories I can now tell are a reflection from the eyes of a savior who saved me, and that savior was me. You are the savior of your life, and only yours. The day I remembered I am the light of the God consciousness, was the day I fell to my knees and wept. I had said the words "I am done," so many times, and yet I was still in the shadows of the dark, waiting to be saved from the misery I believed to be true. Yes, the pain was real, the concrete evidence of hurt was real, the human losses had really happened, and a piece of my heart was dead. But the misery was a choice. The anger a choice. The desire to stay in contracts that had expired and tell stories that no one, not even myself would know the truth to, was all contributing factors to the suffering and misery I chose to continue as if it were a debt I had to pay. From my knees, from my lowest and now defining moments, I surrendered it all and gave it all to the God outside of me, and with this I signed a new contract of love. I am still reading the details and coming to terms with the action steps required to live a life of joy and happiness. It takes work, and you need to do the outside work. There may be magic mushrooms that yes in this crazy journey I tried once in a tea but those show a truth you may not be ready to see and left me with a guilt that would not be serving me. The human experience and interaction without an ego expectation is the experience I shall now live.

Our ultimate contract is to see ourselves as the source of it all and the savior of everything within us. To learn to love, means we reach out and up. To find compassion we share, and to see each other we become kind. The simplicity was lost in the translation of a desire to complicate the wording. The freewill of ego had cast a shadow, and we had the freewill to allow it to be real or to believe that there is always light in the dark.

I had become the master of getting in the first word and the last word of a distorted truth that had no value and was not part of my identity, but a shadow of the fear of losing it again this time around. Today I woke to the realization of the contracts, including the one with myself to not stab the voice of my own echo, but to allow it to flow without frustration to the ears ready to receive its messages. Now, in an "ah ha" moment of realization, I understand that the echo is the vibration of my heart, and by stabbing my throat I was actually stabbing my heart. I had fucking hired myself as my own hit man, and with a contract to constantly sabotage my own life and silence a voice that was a gift from the source of it all.

I had been soul contracted to my parents, as they were soul contracted to me. Under human contract, we often have a return or void clause in the deal, but thankfully that option is not available within soul contracts. I mean who else would have ruined my life if it were not for parents? Oh yes, Me! I could do that without even blinking an eye. As the story continues, it is one of a pleaser, an impulse, and the power of saying "no." An intentional story that needed boundaries and a true story of the love which has endured it all. For the biggest contract was the line that said, "We would love each other forever and always." What if you looked at your life as a series of contracts and when they are done it is over? Then as easy as a snap of the fingers, a new contract begins.

The contract that broke me was the beginning of my second salon, and this chapter cannot be told without the credit due to my mother. She gave me the push and kick in the ass to start this business and with a desire to share cost and space we had planned to combine our own individual businesses under one roof. But in my truth, I had been slowly planning to open the second salon, from a place of putting things together in a healthy way. I was carefully taking the time to get prepared so that when it opened, I would be ready for the crazy ass world, instead of opening with a moment that was projected from fear and frustration. Things did not unfold the way I had envisioned.

The story of the second salon is hard to tell, along with many others, as many of them are very sensitive. You will likely find yourselves in similar situations, where you will have to prepare yourself for the fact that speaking your truth in order to heal, is going to cause discomfort and unintentional hurt in the hearts of those around you. I was uncertain and insecure about telling this story, but it is an important story to tell as it ties directly back into my lack of trust at the time. Contracts, relationships, and commitments all rely heavily on trust and without trust everything will fail. This experience took me to a place where I would trust no one, and I wouldn't be able to tell the story from a place of love, until such a time that I would be ready to learn how to trust again.

It may seem in the beginning of this story that I am questioning the integrity of my mother. However, I assure you that I am not, for as my life is unfolding on the outside, I understand that the movement of *More Than Existing* can't be done by me alone if significant changes in our lives are to occur. This story is in the past where it started from the eyes of a broken thirty-year-old woman. Today, I retell the story from the open heart of a forty-eight-year-old daughter who is so thankful for her mom. By the end of this chapter you will know what happens to good people when the shadows of others come into our life and lay down their blankets of darkness over our minds.

This is the story of a contract, a moment of misjudgment, bad decisions, and a choice to choose a road that leads to a hard lesson. As I was prepping along with my mother and others the new salon offering both of our individual businesses under one roof, in preparation of its grand opening, I entrusted my mother to drop off the completed paperwork required to register the company. My mother at this time had her own company, as I had mine, and both were registered in the same industry, but offering different services. While standing in line waiting to hand over the business registration, my mother had one of her impulsive brilliant ideas, which she assumed would serve us both for the best and took action prior to thinking it through or consulting with me. In this flash impulsive decision, and without my full consent, she decided to make herself a partner in my business, by adding her name to the paperwork and filing the business registration. Returning to the salon, she opened the door, and announced joyfully in front of everyone there that she was now my new business partner!

That day, my mother crossed a boundary and a line that would project a hurt in my heart that I did not realize I had carried for so long. I should have stopped it right there and repaired our relationship, but instead I heard myself saying "Yes," when I should have trusted my heart in knowing that this was not the plan God had for me. It also had not been in the plan to leave my previous job so quickly either, or speed up the launching of the business. I was thankful for the kick in the butt my mother provided, but was not thankful for the push, and as we grew the business I felt myself becoming lost, swallowed up in the shadows with desire and a projection out of vengeance, attached to the anger of the partnership. I found myself out of anger taking from her soul, taking from her power, and taking from parts of me. I was allowing the energy to become angrier instead of having a conversation about how I really felt and acknowledging my feelings that this decision came from a desire within her heart to take from what was mine. In her impulsive decision, she had taken my glow, my light, and shadowed all of it with her hurt of staying within broken relationships.

As the years rolled on like a virus in my body, the anger and hurt became larger as I watched my mother struggle and suffer. I watched as she became angrier, and defeated, and as the energy became depleted, it rolled over our hearts turning it to stone for staying in a relationship that was so horribly uncomfortable. For my mother, the comfort she knew from childhood up to this relationship, and anything in between that was wonderful and made of love, she was sure to push away. As I was trying to bring love, she was pushing the love out. In our social circles are groups of people who are reflections of ourselves, and neither one of us was the reflection of the same. The judgments that came upon me as nobody knew who I was, often came from those she allowed in, for I had built up a stone wall of protection in order to be in the presence of all that was existing in my mother's life. She was choosing to not live a life in her light and was merely just existing in the shadows of her own pain.

Maintaining a 50/50 partnership could not be sustained, as we both had power struggles, tears, and anchors keeping us from compromising. We could not find the balance, and I was already well on my way to drowning in what I thought was functioning depression that nobody could see, for I had carefully selected the perfect mask to wear. Daily I would put on a false face for the world, pretending that "Everything was ok, that I was ok," a well learned condition stemming from both sides of my family. The day I finally broke and declared that I was done, came with a realization that our power struggles could not continue on a week foundation, and one of us would have to walk away. I made the decision to get out, even though it cost me dearly in the sense of all I was leaving behind. She took over the company and I asked for little in return, but I had to save what was left of me. As I look back now, I know my role in the problems, but our pain was too deep, and our ideals and views were too far from meeting in the middle.

At the time I was struggling in my fight of a daughter energy as Crystal Andrus Morissette speaks of in her book "The Emotional Edge." The selfish part of me, the child, did not know enough to know better. She was crying out, screaming, and having tantrums, declaring to be seen as important, to have what was rightfully a place on the throne, but knowing this would never come, and why should it? I was here to be of service. To love, honor and respect a mother many people did not see as a healer and a light who had cared for me. What I had learned through all of this, was that she never viewed me as her daughter, she has placed me in the role of being a sister. I have learned that she was not in a healthy place to become attached and be the emotionally stable mother, but damn, she was a great physical mom.

Looking at our relationship as sisters instead of mother/daughter changes everything as sisters compete and get compared to each other. Sisters is truly what we were! We have played the role of sisters this whole time and even though she loved me from the role as a mother, she brought with it all of her numbed pain and feelings that I could not escape as the mystic and healer within me was always wanting to fix what was not mine to fix. There were parts of her that never attached to my sensitive but fiery essence.

We had become sisters, and the contract that she signed was one where we would both learn a valuable lesson and realize the blessing that had transpired in placing us together. The story of the business contract and the fear of lack, losing, or one having more than the other, was never meant to have been. This was a story and a contract about devotion and resilience, that in the end cost us both everything, but also where we gained everything! The magic of the family we built along with the empire, became a place of giving, a place for people to gather when they had nowhere to go. The place was simply magical, and my mother and I were the resilience to the magic behind it all. We gave our all and from our hearts we loved. We opened the door to everyone seeking beauty, as if they were family, just as a sister would do, and as the contracts for service kept coming in so did the makings of a sisterhood. As representatives of the empire, we always showed up with all our broken and put together pieces, sometimes fighting in front of clients and friends but this was the weakness of a foundation and the sadness in the fairytale. Sometimes the fights became ugly as we acted like two broken children fighting for the same thing, ultimately wanting to succeed together and grow together, but built on weak personal foundations that weren't strong enough to maintain a healthy relationship.

My mother is truly a fantastic mother to both myself and my brother and to so many others, but she was also a broken child who did not have the mother that she needed. She carries a sadness from a painful past, and stories that she has yet to tell. These are her stories to share when the time is right, but I can share that she has known poverty, pain, cheating, alcoholism, and everything in between. She has ultimately only wanted to protect me, but in her desire to protect, she exposed me.

I have a contract with my own daughter of strength, just as my mother did, and the mothers before her. I have made the same mistakes, but in that contract, I have seen the circle, and today, the cycle of the circle ends!

I had chosen to try to do the same safe thing for my daughter from the shutdown three-year-old in myself, as each of us ultimately try to do the best we can on our weak foundations. From where I am today and the foundation I have repaired with care and quality, I can say I signed my own contract, and within have placed an oath. "I honor my mother and love her with all my awareness and without ownership of her own actions and behaviors. I place a crown of love on her head, one that she fully deserves. She is the matriarch of my family and I do not just love her, I respect her for the journey she has had to endure. She instilled the confidence in me that she never had for herself, and my resistance was in the selfless action of her always trying to give me her light that I would refuse, for I knew it was hers to shine.

I will be in the years to come the matriarch of my own family and I will lead with my staff just as Jesus, Moses, Saint Anne, Mother Mary and all who have walked with dignity and integrity before me. With strength and determination just as my mother has, and compassion and kindness as my heavenly Father has always shown and provided me. I will write my code of ethics and live by a truth I know to be true. I'll lead with inspiration and as I have learned from the books of "Lead Like Jesus," I will lead among my people, and we will always hand over the keys to open doors of possibilities. Our family is your family, but I will always be aware of my personal family's needs and never will I be a sister to compete with, for I have forever made a promise to let my daughter shine and grow in her own light, guiding as a mother of love and compassion.

My own daughter is both beauty and love and glows in a light I did not push her to be in. Never intentionally stepping in to shadow her, but I take back what I didn't do and that was to always be there emotionally for I was conditioned to shut down and now I am awake and feeling it all. I will never run from her pain again or infuse my stories onto her moments. She is the strength that has become the mirror reflection of the greatness of myself, my mother, my grandmothers and grandfathers, my dad, my brother, and those who choose to be in her life as they were contracted to mine.

As the next generation is about to arrive, I can say that this contract will be one of faith, hope, and love. I have looked into my granddaughter's eyes before and I know this one is arriving to be the princess who will claim her throne in due time, as a change and a light that has been seen with a knowing that we are all precious gifts to be cared for with love. I gained so many valuable lessons from my ancestors and this world, and just as they walked ahead of me to take the burdens of the growing pains of an evolving world and the human species, I have no regrets that I follow in their footsteps. For that I now say "Thank you" for having the courage to not give up, and for the gifts they gave me.

Today I have set all free including myself, of the terms of contract I thought I knew, but as I master my way through this life I now live as if I know nothing. I have forty-eight years of experience and a tapped in ability that has blessed me with this life and for that I say, "Thank you." My only new contract with myself is to live a life of what I had been seeking. To live as the best human I can be and that is all that shall be asked of you. As I am coming closer to the end of the words, I graciously share with all who have been open to the desired intention of loving healing, and I ask for all that each word and page be blessed. My contract to commit to this book is ending and the stories will fade into the nonexistent past. As I look to the future, I ask of you to not be afraid to sign a new contract with yourself and live a life of *More Than Existing*.

CHAPTER 14

The value of your identity

REVERTING HAS BECOME A PROCESS that has brought the most awareness to the journey of writing. Saying enough of the right things and not using filler words as we do in life, had become a habit for my words and my story to be enough. I know for myself and others, I have remembered my biggest gift and how I used it to create the image of a perfect life.

Creativity has always been my biggest gift, and that I have not said up until writing this sentence. From hair to make-up, I helped change the world for women even if just for one day. The reward was in the eyes, and the smile reflecting back filled my heart, as we revamped the beauty that the world around was sucking out, as if the energy vampires had taken the identity and left the disillusioned belief of a faceless presence looking back in the mirror. Transformation would be like refilling the fuel running through the veins until life was restored.

After years of being lost in the stories, the glimpses of beauty are reminders that until we are ready to take back the identity, we can feel but are yet to see. As I think of how many times, I had let myself become faceless and forgettable, there is an anger raging inside my soul, screaming in the hopes that someone hears the cry for help. Cry's from a human who had become an emotional punching bag, a dumping station for the hurt that was oozing from the pores of another, all because she was seeking the love she believed was not there.

Today as I am in a state of thawing out from the twenty plus years of being frozen and numb, I feel myself actually feeling and an anger is brewing. I had reverting back and started this chapter, as I guess was intended, back to the beginning of seeking answers to my "how" and "why?" I was reverting, and from my old viewpoint starting to give credit where it was not due, apologizing to the people in the stories, even though 90% of those reading would never know who they are. Some of you may know a piece of the stories, but no one knows the truth, except those who have been left to wear the wounds.

After writing twenty pages explaining and apologizing for the behaviors and habits of others, you may feel this story is about you! If so then I am doing my job very well, in having the words of my story reflect the truths of yours. In so many ways, I am like a turtle going through life at a slow and steady pace, sometimes trapped on my back as I process challenges, but persevering none the less.

I had made a choice to go inward and snoop around the mind and body that had become old before it's time, reminiscing on the past, but trying not to relive stories of what had once been but had since died. I had already lived these stories once and did not have to do that shit again, even if some of those moments were glorious. If you try returning to it, it will be painful, like trying to put an air mattress back in its original box. You are not the person you were yesterday, so you cannot expect to be who you were twenty years ago.

As I witness so many trying to hang on to past relationships and experiences, trapped in the misery of warped stories that have stayed on repeat, I sense and see a desperation and fear of a world that is yet to exist. I am going to honor this chapter and those that I love, but god damn it, I am human, and there is just some that even at the end I may not be ready to forgive. My loyalty is loyal to a fault. My trust is developing, and I can tell you in the beginning of the process I did not even trust myself. My worth and value I traded off as cheap wine for a moment of satisfaction over the lips of the unworthy, and yes that is in the next book!

I was conditioned to believe that bad behavior was to be acceptable, and not to deal with the real issues. Today, I can tell you, I deal with my shit. Like any habit it has not been an easy one to break when you are continually trying to insert a "but" and justification from the mouth of the enabling. I am aware the stories I tell may be viewed differently by another who may have also contributed to the story line, but I finally have compassion for my truth and a desire to surrender it all. Chalk it up to the remake of stories we love to hate and hate to lose. For who are we without a story? Who would you be if you had no story?

I was filled with stories, deceits, and halfhearted truths. The victim of a lifetime of angry words projected at me through the repeat of, "You are just like....." or, "go take your pills." With no regard for the pain I endured through the years of grieving a mother I watched give her all to others but not to me, and the men that I gave my all to just to see peace in their cold, but warm hearts, I would over time erode to an unrecognizable glob of my stature.

I am a mother who gives my all, because my parents kept the family together, no matter the storm, for way too many years through their dedication to fight for a cause. That dedication to myself and my sibling was to be admired. Now, as grandparents they shine apart, but together I gained the understanding that it was never too late to be what we could not be in the younger years. A pleaser and workaholic became badges I wore so well that I worked my physical self to death, for a satisfaction that would never come. A lesson I was slow to learn, but now I get it! In my present state, I labelled myself the "Kept woman of leisure," as a return to my faith has provided me the space to heal, along with the blessings to connect with others whom I guide and heal. I am a kept woman. Kept safe in the arms of God to fall apart and rise up to an identity I now see with love in the mirror reflection. A beautiful face with eyes that can see myself in others with love and compassion.

As I found myself at the root of the problem, I had to take a good look at my life and the roles that I had played. Reflecting back to it all, I am now lovingly aware of my weaknesses and character flaws, so when the assholes come calling, I take a good look in the mirror to see if I have reverted back to the asshole in me. If you are for one moment questioning yourself, maybe take a good look in the mirror and ask, "Is what I am seeing in them any reflection of something inside of me?" If your answer is no, then you have a freewill right to use your fuck off pass!

The gates that opened to bring me into this world were to be honored and appreciated, as the walls that held me safe were also the walls of the woman who had been so guarded that she could not see her glow. Her desire to be anything but her mother became the reflection she would show me, and I was afraid to be a mother. The healer in me could feel the wounded healer in her, and the wounded healer in her mother cost her a fear of mothering, which consumed her glow.

As I sit in a place of grace at the gates of God with a golden key and an opportunity to open the next doors. I feel blessed to be experiencing this moment. I think back with gratitude and love for the strength my mother has shown and instilled in me. As I go further back in this book, I could tell stories of how a little girl felt alone and unloved, but those were stories through the eyes of a child who was still living in the adult I had become today. Those stories trailed my life and became the projection of all that would transpire in my choices to turn from the brink of my own self destruction. I travelled to the shadows and allowed the doors to the golden opportunities to close, as

I would give the keys to my heart to the undeserving and the ones who through their eyes, I could see my unworthiness. I have so many stories to tell of pain, but I have also discovered my worth through the eyes and stories of my ancestors as they have channeled back through me as a medium and physical medium over the years. I must have felt over 1000 years of pain, but I was shown tremendous value in remembering the moments and people who have inspired me, taught me valuable lessons, and showed me through watching suffering spread like a virus, that keeping the skeletons in the closet serves no one as it only protects the evil and destroys the innocent. This I know all too well, as I spent years living in frustration until I learned to value myself and stay true to me by choosing to live vulnerable, open, and real. This decision is now a personal choice and I am not judging anyone for not wanting to share their stories, because the stories of you are none of my business, and it's your right to choose what to share if anything.

There comes a time when to be true to you, you may not only have to let go of the past, but also let go of those who do not serve your soul, including sometimes, family. We have been conditioned to believe that family sticks together, but when there are holes in a sinking ship, and no one is willing to repair it, you will have to jump ship in order to save yourself. Trust me, I may see through the eyes of love, but eyes of love never mean sacrificing yourself to be liked. I have learned the hard way that I am not the product of my past, I am not here to try to make anyone like me, but I am here to live a life of love.

Create boundaries, because you love yourself too much to allow the toxins of those not awakened to infest you and your light. The value placed on me depends on my voice, my words, and staying true to my integrity. It is fine to have compassion from a distance.

I remember my mother telling me that as a child she would take the pennies off the eyes of the deceased in the Catholic

Church to go buy the candies that the other kids had, because she was too poor. I do not know how much truth there is to that story, but know she had to do things in order to survive that a child should never have to endure.

I remember we always chuckled at her many stories and escapades, but also felt her pain. The woman she is today would return a penny she found on the ground. Her integrity and code of ethics in her adult years would never take from another human dead or alive to give to herself first. But now through her desire to give to another first, it has become a quality that has depleted her. Looking at her story now, I think maybe those pennies were a gift from heaven. A gift from the eyes that could not see through the human, but could see through the spirit, that those children were in need of some moments of happiness, and through their shame they would chuckle as a response to the trauma. No one knows, but I understand that her humor over the years has been used to cover up the pain, and I have been conditioned to do the same. Those pennies taken as a child, I know have been replaced many times over as she gave to others. As an adult, I do not condemn the behavior of those children, nor do I judge. For I have come to understand that as I have walked in the shoes of judgement in the past, there were times when the luxury of shoes was one my mother did not even have.

I have placed judgement upon myself, and even when provided an opportunity of riches, I would claim to not be worthy enough to succeed. I was a rich kid with a poverty brain and that was hard to lose. Learning to say, "I am worthy, and I matter" have been the hardest to accept. The past few years, at the peak of it all, the human commodity dried up and the hard done by child appeared once again. I was sitting on a gold mind of death and knowledge that was not mine. But just as my mother had lived in fear of the rich, so had I, and the worth of my identity would steal from the eyes of those who would show me riches, and like a thief in the night I would rob myself of a life.

As I look back at my journey, from that place where I sat with my golden key waiting for the opportunity to open the next door, I know I will never again let the next opportunity escape out of a fear to succeed, or from the false reality and truth of illusions of the old stories. It was from those moments in a story of having no shoes and taking the pennies, that the stories of poverty and pain projected onto her became her why and her desire to take from her own mouth to feed us first. She would give her last penny to make sure myself, my sibling, and all the children she took care of had enough, she had pre-paid that debt of those pennies she took from the eyes of the deceased, a thousand times over. From this place in my heart and in my life, I may speak of the stories of our disagreements or our moments of pain, but my love and respect for the woman who came through it all, acknowledges that her walls were to protect the inner child in her. I have released and surrendered the suffering. I Corrie, who suffered in pain, made a choice to free myself and as I was set free, I surrounded my mother in love, setting her free to free herself.

As my mother was freed, so were her stories and the entrapment of protection. She now sits at the place of her own glory, in a life that she is now adjusting to. Collecting retirement for her doors of opportunities have passed, but her door to sit in her chair on her throne as the queen of our world, is hers to now claim. Just as I had in my awakened dreams placed the crown upon the head of Jesus, I now placed on my mother her crown. But this crown is one of glory, for her pains and struggles we have all had to endure, as had her granddaughter, but for my mother, and the many years we spent working beside each other I am blessed.

I am honored to stand before her and crown her the queen of my world, for she is not a woman who wears a title nor is she a woman too proud to say she was ever wrong. She is a woman who wears her boots well tied to still be on the run, but still manages to laugh and make fun of us and herself every opportunity that she has. Without these women or the men, I have walked my life with, I would not be able to write this story, nor would I be here to live in the glow. The glow started with those parents, with a love that may not of been able to stand the test of time, but a love they created and the love that we have in our hearts as brother and sister and into our families.

The generations to come will have the opportunity to handle the golden key, but we have learned to not give them ours, but to give them their own. For the key that unlocks my heart, may not fit in the heart of my daughter or my granddaughter, but a custom key with its own glow will definitely fit in their hearts. I travel back but do not stay in the past for too long now, as it is all just chapters. The stories of a beautiful future is where I place my dreams.

I have allowed my creativity to flow and become both awakened and enlightened to all that my forty-eight years have provided to experience. I have walked the journey and accepted the gifts I have been given, not letting anything go to waste as I designed a life. I have learned from the Creator that the greatest gift I was given was to be human, and I value the identity of the human that my gifted, creative self has molded and shaped into the form of my own life. I have experienced and learned more in this lifetime because I have truly absorbed and listened, realizing that I have never really just existed, but have been evolving.

I recall standing on the beaches of my aboriginal family roots, and that of the hunters and gathers, witnessing the stories of beauty but also the stories of slaughter and pain, caused by the ego of mankind. To identify by anything other than spirit is saddening, as I look across the water and down at the beautifully eroded rocks. As I pause in this moment, I remembered to breathe, and vow to live and do better. I gaze at those beautiful smooth rocks that have been there since the beginning of time and can feel the energy of the water as if it has become my emotions. The waves washing emotions through me, a representation of the water becoming the body. We will always have moments that roll in to wash over our hearts, moments that help us let go so we may breathe again. We will always be in the ebb and flow of the tides that roll over us, reshaping the landscape and changing the view.

As I glance at the stones beneath my bare feet, I can feel the hardness and the pain become real, just as it will when we stay in any uncomfortable place for too long. But still I stayed, savoring the beauty before my eyes. Finally, when I was ready, I walked back to stand at the banks of the ocean, once again feeling the comfort of something new. In this moment of softness and comfort surrounding my feet, I realized that I will never again have to stand in the discomfort to enjoy the view. The grass is truly greener on the other side, and yes, the view changes when you go to higher ground! When we become our own savior, and we realize the truth of our worth, the perspective of the identity becomes ours to claim. You have made it this far! Imagine what will be possible as you remain faithful until the very end!

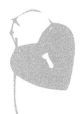

CHAPTER 15

The beginning of the end

COMING TO THE END OF creating the first book in the *More Than Existing* series and the realization of the desire to write from where I had been, brings me right back to the beginning, to the truth that I need to go return to the beginning of time. Back to the creation of all, to the Big Bang, to the light of God, to whatever you want to call it. To the essence of the source of the breath that we take in and the light within us all. This reference I will argue with no one, for we simply will never know the whole story of a past that does not exist.

As I find myself holding a draft copy of this book you now read in my hand for the first time, I feel the truth of my story and the weight of parts of my life in a new form. As it became heavier and heavier, I realized how heavy life can be when we move away from faith, trust, and hope. When we lose all essence of our truth to the darkness of the shadow, we lose our light to the ego. As I started to rebuilt my connection to the God conscious within me, I was taken back to the beginning of my human life, to the days I slept with a bible under my pillow and prayed to the angels I knew to be real.

I found myself placed in a Pentecostal school, churches, and Sunday school, learning the word of God mixed with the human versions and egos that would also come with it. As I found myself being a victim of the circumstances of the past and conditioned to believe the shadows of others, I would start to doubt the truth of my own existence. As I felt my life crumbling during that time and a need to reach out, I discovered I was also reaching up to the Source I thought had abandoned me for my wrong doings that I just could not get right. I chose a relationship with a man of no faith and to live in fear of speaking my truth, following a path of prosecution. I prayed in silence and hid the truth that something was stirring inside of me, but my truth I could not hide. I had discovered I was a channel and an unexpected and humble meeting with Mother Mary and Jesus on the cross became the "why," to the whole reason I knew I would have to walk this journey. In 2009, I wrote a statement that I knew was as if I wrote a creed, declaring that "I will live a life of *More Than Existing!*"

God has a funny way of fooling us, and I truly believed I was waiting for this big moment as this was the prize at the end of the journey I was going to take. Instead my truth became that I was being taken on the journey of realizing our soul purpose is to awaken to the fact that we are here to live, love, and honor our human. My purpose at this point was learning to laugh, as the human needed to laugh, and the humans in my life that care for me also had the same human experiences I have had, whether they were a parent, grandparent, aunt, or uncle. It didn't matter, for they were also children at some point and had been conditioned to believe the truth they had left, but also to believe in their worth based on the beliefs and conditions of others. I had created a full 6 month *More Than Existing* self-actualization coaching program and it was not until I created the second level, *Existing Beyond The Reflection,* that I learned to see the truth. I was hiding behind my spirituality and channel because it was safe, but I was still not believing in the human, just like when I was a kid hiding behind my mother's legs, and just like my mother, my channel, Mary Ellen kicked me out! Even with all the knowledge and wisdom my human world had taught me I was still afraid that I was not enough! Do not worry if you also find yourselves in this same place, as sometimes it is like a slow release, followed by a knock on the head that awakens us! At this point in my journey, to add in even more humor, I was taken all the way back to the old faith prior to organized religion.

It was shown to me on this journey, that even the biblical stories I had heard were based on stories repeated throughout time, built, and told from humans who were not telling their own story. In my version, I looked beyond the illusions of the truths that were told to cause fear, to cause us to believe in something that was ego-based, and I looked to the humans such as Jesus, Mother Mary, Moses, Abraham, Mary Magdalene and all of the above in the holy realms. To see their stories through the eyes of God within me, to find love and compassion and to see that the book of Moses was for me to discover through my own desire to find love within. That my code of ethics and my integrity was strongly based upon that gut feeling of knowing what was right and what was wrong and knowing that fear could not be the projection of my future nor can it be that of yours.

I looked at the women such as Mary Magdalene and considered how that story would be told if repeated from the eyes of a man who wanted to diminish the light of a woman, or even a woman telling the story of a man that she was angry with who was not conforming to what she wanted him to be. I looked at the poison we would spread and the toxins we would allow to form within ourselves when our wants, needs, and desires were not being met. I discovered through my relationship with Jesus, that during my claim to fame title of calling myself "a good girl," I had become a pleaser and I had laid myself on a cross to be victim to the judgment of others and to take the punishments. I myself would not create my truth, but instead would allow my reputation to be built through the words of others, as if they were building my empire. But they did not know me, or my truth!

As you have now looked at your own life and explored your own journey through my words and my writings, I hope you were able to see the times when you have sacrificed yourself for the happiness of others, and feel no desire to do that again. As you reflect on any pain or suffering that you may have endured, do you see the times where you have nailed yourself to the problems or to the struggles? Times where others have nailed you to their problems, making you responsible for their life and for everything that has transpired, as if you were the cause! This had been a common occurrence in my life because I had allowed it. Now, from where I am today, and at the beginning once again, I am moved beyond a life of just existing and am now living true to myself. This book, my journey was never about Jesus, God, or Mother Mary, it also had nothing to do with angels. It truly started with a desire to stop the anger and the pain that had caused me to be weighed down in physical pain, obesity, unhappiness, financial problems, and all the human existence was taking over within my life. Like a virus I was infected with shadows and my light I could not see.

The unhealthiest relationship I was having was the one with myself and I wanted to blame it on everyone else, as I was not ready to take responsibility for my own life. I am not saying that others did not cast the shadows over onto me and cause me pain, as you can well see in this book that has also happened. I had to go back to the basics and allow the old stories to die. To sit with the human and say "I am sorry, I did not see you, or my value, but today I am here sitting with you and today we will start the process if you so choose."

This journey has taken me to the darkened soul, to the essence of my shadows, in order to recognize that little Corrie had taken a stand as a child, but had forgotten that she had the power to stand up, to speak a truth, and have a voice to say "No!" To know that she was safe in most places of her life, but a moment in time had left her feeling unsafe and everyone else became the victim of the sadness and despair. I had to learn to look at the eyes of those who lent me theirs, to look at the child within a man and know that we have all been a victim of something, sadly some more severe than others, but still traumatic and needing love and attention. We have all been a survivor and a survivalist. We have all been a little narcissist, and most of all, we came from the light.

Our soul, our spirit, was never in need of repair, as it has always been of pure form. The humans had the issues and from this point onwards I made a choice to live in the joy and happiness, making a commitment to not run away from somebody else's pain, but to hold space as we all will have to endure the human feelings of loss, grief, death, and rebirth. A commitment to be present as we go through destruction and dismantling in order to restructure and rebuild a life that is now built on a foundation stronger than ever, as it has been build out of love, compassion, kindness and without divide. For the dismantling of the old foundations could not be sustained.

The death of the old, the beginning of the new, are words I have used in sessions and spoke of within myself, but truly did not get until now. I did not understand until after a weekend of letting go of this spiritual healer, letting go of any expectations, and just being present in the experience and moments that had occurred in my life. I was receiving attention due to a beauty I could not see, and struggling through only wanting to be seen as the glowing spiritual self, all while realizing it was in fear of not wanting to behave as my old self would have, or behaving as I had watched my parents do before me.

Even though I was not cheating, opportunities arrived that gave me chances to experience a part of me that would have been totally acceptable to my old self. I was teaching my twenty-two-year-old the value of maintaining her own integrity and grabbing onto something that was alive within herself. In teaching, I realized that I had also passed a little insecurity onto her, just as my mother had passed on to me. I recognized that she also could not see the external beauty that glowed from her, and her amazing unique look. I had unknowingly taught her that our bigger than a size two body, was not attractive or was still needing to be perfected. I had come to a point, a pivotal turning point where my past had trickled into my world, into my life once again, causing me to question if this was a true part of the death or now part of my rebirth? There is a fine line between what we take with us and what we leave behind, a truth in knowing that there is an unknown, but familiar sense of our lives we are living now, and the future we are allowing to be created for us when we make a choice to step not aside but beyond. Taking a leap does not mean moving to the side or standing back, it is to leap so far ahead that you wobble as you land. Unsure of your footing you sway from side to side, as if you have to contemplate the stillness and back and forth movement. You feel a pull to fall back and a fear to fall forward, all while knowing to breathe in, tighten your core, and bend your knees to ground and steady yourself. To once again be present in the sense that you have arrived.

Rebirth does not come with a clear view of the future or a manual, it comes with signs and synchronicity. It comes with ah ha moments you just have to be paying attention to see what is in a moment, an introduction, and an interaction. It is about the awareness of knowing it is your first experience in the newness, the new you. It is the moments of being kind to yourself when you feel you have missed a moment, but did you? Most times the moment was just not ripe and ready for you, but the world has taught us to believe we missed it, and we find ourselves slipping back into the old patterns that we left in the death. These are the "beat yourself up" moments. The "what the hell is wrong with me?" belief. In truth, there is nothing wrong with the moment that you did not get. There is a greater awareness in the fact that you just needed a memory to allow you to achieve the most out of the moment when it would rise again, and you would breathe in the ever expanding beauty and confidence to walk in the grace that was always present, but not ready for the you that would be comfortable enough to walk in the presence of Source and the life you had been blessed to receive in full expansion.

I have just walked to the end of the world as I have known it. I have walked to the root of my ancestors, my past and the many dimensions my spirit has lived in and seen where I shall settle in peace. I surrendered into the unsafe space of my mind and my heart and let go of the roots. I proclaimed my prophecies that I would die young, with a truth and conviction of faith I let go. That day I died. I had been wearing the old self as a coat of protection, protecting the gift that in many times I may have been killed for, a realization that many have died the same in this life with judgement, shame, and facing those trying to change, shut up or shut down the healer, the witch, the feminine, the prophet, and the light.

Many years of fear and hiding had pushed me into survival mode but strength, faith, and love has taken me on this journey to the end, where I could let go of the root, honor the ancestors, and let it all die. To awaken empty, bathe my feet in the water of life and death, and begin a journey back home, for I am now safe to walk in the dark of the unknown. With faith in the light, power to be free, and room to expand, for my day of death will come again but also too shall I rise.

Do not miss the journey out of conditioned fear. Be bold, be brave and let go of the root! For you, my friends are here to embrace the journey, die a thousand deaths and be reborn to a thousand more. You are here to learn, trust and believe in magic. To know, learn and share love, and most of all you are here to *More Than Exist*!

CHAPTER 16

The cycle may break, but the circle shall never be broken

I WOKE TODAY TO THE end of the suffering I had endured. It has not been forgotten, but my anger has found a voice and just as Moses did, my staff has hit the earth and I can feel the waters parting as I now say once again, "I am done!"

I now walk worthy with a conviction and a desire to be the woman in the red boots, with a passion in my steps as I have walked the golden road of brick and mortar. I have fallen deeply in love with my shadows, and from here on in I vow to not make the bad behaviors of others, including myself, be acceptable.

I have claimed my strength, courage, heart, and remembered that I had a brain beyond the ancient wisdom of the lives I have lived before. Claiming my name as the white light and cutting off the darkness of those who had tried to darken the light, I now know to be the beauty within that had been radiating out.

I walk now through the parted waters and to the other side, as I have experienced the crippling and not so pretty death of my old self. I walked out of the turtle shell and from the other side I dare not look back with any desire to return. I am the reflection of all that is of and beyond the reflection, the artist and creator in me who became the savior of myself, is now holding the mirror in front of who I have become to reflect back to you, so you can see what is beyond the truths and lies you have told yourself. That you to can walk beyond the existence and with the journey of *More Than Existing* completed I have fulfilled the contract of commitment that I had perfected for others, but until the end of *More Than Existing* I had not committed to me!

I half assed the job of healing and laid an unconscious decision to lay that responsibility upon another. I had fallen to my knees more times then I care to remember, and as I dropped for the last time, I prayed to the God above and not to the God within me. I had to reach for the magic and the belief in miracles that would all be heard when I was to fully let go of my suffering. What was to unfold in just a few weeks was to awaken me to a reflection I had yet to see but now shall never forget. Today, and every day I remember I am golden and some days I am fucking golden! Are you ready to be golden?

All had to fall away, and I mean all, to allow my own deception to be set free. I walked the path these past few months with bossy St. Anne as she guided me to a statue made of gold and asked, "Now do you understand golden?" Today, I can finally declare that "Yes, I do." As I saw Jesus as he laid in the safe arms of Mother Mary, in the state of death, I knew the story that was to die was the pain of the son, I had carried as if he were alive. I was never to seek the punishment I laid upon myself but was to weep through my grief. I had been the one I did not trust, and my question of worth was I could not understand, why me? Today as I look back, I now know the truth, and please allow me to end this book with a truth that takes us full circle and back to the essential need for me! The cycles that are broken straighten the circle and then we have the will and freedom to heal.

As I remembered the woman I had started to fall in love with, but slowly losing on this journey again, I now know she too will have to leave. For I now declare, "Look out world" for the grace I shall now walk in, having discovered the value of my purpose is to be the best human I can be! I tried too many times to give my life away, to fix other people, give them the healthy shakes, the healthy food, the healthy everything.

As I finish writing the first chapter of the second book in *More Than Existing - Beyond The Reflection*, the morning after I completed the first book, I was about to celebrate with bacon and eggs and I heard, "Go back to the essentials." I had gone through the process of losing the weight, but in the process of gaining me, I have gained back ten pounds. Ok, let's be honest, I actually came back twenty. See, another story I believed to be true as I found myself wanting to believe that I was so much more content in a little chubbier body. But in truth it was the return of the protection as I had experienced an invasion up on my body, by allowing the anger to go inwards instead of outwards. The protection became heavier and deeper as I had to sit and relive the past, write the stories, and then rewrite them again from a place of love. I had to remember the past pain, while living in some of the happiest times in my life. I had to fall in love with who I had become before I could be the change I wanted to see.

This morning I woke up and as that staff hit the ground, I knew one more time "I am done!" I am not responsible for the suffering of others nor will I allow myself to suffer again including with weight that holds my body down. Instead of the bacon and eggs, I went back to a bag of Arbonne shakes that have been sitting in my cupboard, periodically drinking a shake here and there, as I was slowly regressing and returning to the body I did not want to see, and not that I didn't love her, she just was not for me. I could not carry her and myself into the future.

Time and time again I had packed up that bag of shake powder and the new bag that was sitting beside it. I gave some to my partner to try and help him become healthy, and today I decided I would start again on the journey to take off the twenty pounds. I had just finished a conversation with my daughter about all that had ended and announced I was done with the first book. The past was done, the lotus flower moments of awakening and the dream that had transpired a few days before as I let go of everything. I discovered the essential part of my life was going to be me. I opened the bag and as I scooped out the last two scoops, I started to laugh as the bag was empty, a perfect representation of my journey to truly being done. I drank the last of the old product bag called "essentials," and placed a brand-new bag on the counter, glancing back at the reflection in the mirror and seeing a flashback of the woman I have fallen in love with.

She was dressed in a pink dress with a bronze tan body, her long flowing hair was filled with extensions as her own hair had fallen out drastically from the surgery and she just did not care. She went to the solution instead of the problem and added in hair. She had been on her way to a concert with friends and damn she knew she look good. As a limo pulled up outside she heard the little boy next door ask if she was a Rockstar and yes, yes she was a Rockstar in that moment, the star of her own show, of loving what she was seeing in the mirror but more than that, beyond the mirror.

Reflecting back, I was seeing Tina Turner, Cher, and Leather Tuscadora, all looking back at me along with the Cinderella who had found her gown. In Corrie style the gown was not long and did not flow, it was a mini skirt, soft, beautiful, casual, hot, and of course worn with a shirt that showed a little cleavage, topped off with a bling of gold wrapped around her neck. I strutted my claim to fame hot legs and walked with the strut of a woman on a mission. For the first time she smiled a real smile and remembered her worth. I am not searching for her again and I did not lose her, I still see her.

I am now searching for the health that maintains and holds up the empire. As the foundation has now become strong, it has to withstand the weather of the storms that will come. I will be in the eye of the storm once again but now I have the essential tools of faith, hope, determination to always look beyond the moment, and to remember that I am worthy.

As I stood at the front of the stage, I rocked it out and knew the stage would become mine to own in the days and years to come. For God had a plan and this time I was not losing the essentials of me to those in the shadows, for the only shadow coming through my light would be my own, as I would allow my love to heal the parts of myself that I will no longer allow to be the leader of my light. I am essential to the creation and God told me he has a plan. My role is to prepare for the role with health and vitality. This life is about action steps and you and only you can be the one to take the first step.

Today it is essential that you become the Rockstar of your life, for what the world needs now is love! To have love, we have to release the pain, and I had been the creator of my pain. In truth, it was not the circumstances, but my actions and choices to suffer in misery instead of heal in love. Today I learned the ultimate level of love as I was told to push the boundaries. Today I learned the infinite truth that there is truly no beginning, and no end. The circle of life continues and as I am proudly holding up an ultrasound picture of the circle in our life, my first granddaughter, I have come to the truth of so many things I have spoken and written of.

My desire to be number one is impossible because there is always someone coming to take your place, and that to shall be fine because someday the only first is the return to spirit where everything just is, and nothing has an ego. I have learned everything you are seeking truly is in you and the only one deceiving me had been me. As I tell this last story please sit in a place of peace and allow your pieces to unfold, as your years upon this earth now that you have arrived here are about the return to creation and the awe of living in creation.

February 7th, 2020 I would now finally complete the book with a morning Facebook reminder, four years to the day, when

I made a scary post stating I was leaving my thirty year career to take the journey I was called to do. I could not understand, but with a faith in a God I could not see, I began to search for the source of it all. As I will take this full circle, I will end back at the top, to the moment of truth and the ability to be deceived by the shadow I had trusted, as it's a part of me. Today I now trust as I set myself free and the lesson of trust came back in the eyes of me. Through the truth of my first meeting with Jesus, I could see an unexplained ladder that at the time I could not understand, until today when in a moment of clarity, the truth would become clear.

Only after I let go of the source of my pain could I heal and clearly see the ladder I had been standing on all along. I was now at the top and fully understood that I was still clinging to the crown of thorns I had been asked to place on the head of the beautiful Jesus who looked at me with love and compassion. My fear of hurting anyone was too powerful to believe in the trust and the truth I controlled, and with the freewill I was shown what a life of continually holding the crown of the suffering will do to the soul. I had lived in the disillusioned truth that I had already placed the crown back, but in all reality, I had been holding it all along. Today and only today, after I had given voice to the anger and told my truth, did I finally set my child free. I am now really, truly doing what had been asked of me. I am trusting the process and the guide He shall be.

I can't explain why me, but as I was cleaning house and celebrating the win of the completion of this book, a YouTube video that I have never heard before started to automatically play from my phone. The video was of my mentor Dr. Wayne Dyer, who I have known to be by my side so many times along this journey. I had just finished writing chapter 3 of *Beyond the Reflection* the second book in the *More Than Existing* series and received a message from him that made complete sense of the ladder in my vision placed in front of Jesus. This message gave me the chapter I felt was yet to be written, "Pain is proof of self-deception" was the title! I started to laugh, dance, and cry all at the same time!

I had been at the top of the ladder with nowhere else to go, but my desire to not trust the process of giving over my pain to the man who sacrificed himself to rid us of our suffering allowed me through his eyes to walk back through. Safe enough to be never fully lost but reminded of the burdens that would come in the misery of the pain. I have been set free and today from the place of a love I can only explain as nothing but everything, can I feel the joy and happiness that I asked to seek. For today the miracle has been the end of my suffering and today I have been set free. Are you ready to set yourself free?

Start with the truth but sit at the top of the pain and not in the misery. My truth has now come, and I now claim my own crown of love, the one I was always eager to give away. I see its one of beauty and grace, a little slanted and has a little glow, invisible to the world but clear to the reflection beyond the mirror of life. Today the suffering ends as today my truth sets me free.

Today and only today, as my staff (my human self) hit the ground, did I feel the rumble and complete what had been asked, pushing down that crown and with a faith and a trust finally declare, "I am done!"

CPSIA information can be obtained
at www.ICGtesting.com
Printed in the USA
BVHW032122280820
587568BV00004B/18/J